The Sea Was

The Sea Was My Last Chance

Memoir of an American
Captured on Bataan in 1942
Who Escaped in 1944 and Led
the Liberation of Western Mindanao

DONALD H. WILLS
with Reyburn W. Myers

McFarland & Company, Inc., Publishers
Jefferson, North Carolina, and London

The present work is a reprint of the library bound edition of The Sea Was My Last Chance: Memoirs of an American Captured on Bataan in 1942 Who Escaped in 1944 and Led the Liberation of Western Mindanao, *first published in 1992 by McFarland.*

LIBRARY OF CONGRESS CATALOGUING-IN-PUBLICATION DATA

Wills, Donald H., 1918–
    The sea was my last chance : memoirs of an American
captured on Bataan in 1942 who escaped in 1944 and led the
liberation ofwestern Mindanao / by Donald H. Wills
with Reyburn W. Myers.
        p.   cm.
    Includes index.

    ISBN 978-0-7864-6744-0
    softcover : 50# alkaline paper ∞

    1. Willis, Donald H., 1918– .   2. World War, 1939–1945 —
Campaigns — Philippines — Mindanao Island.   3. World War,
1939–1945 — Prisoners and prisons, Japanese.   4. Escapes —
Philippines — History — 20th century.   5. World War,
1939–1945 — Personal narratives, American.   6. Soldiers —
United States — Biography.   I. Myers, Reyburn Webb, 1921–
II. Title.
D767.4.W55   2011
940.54'26 — dc20   92-50423

BRITISH LIBRARY CATALOGUING DATA ARE AVAILABLE

On the cover: A young Filipino, wounded on Bataan, January 28, 1942, being brought by his comrades to an aid station at Longoskawayan Point (U.S. Army Signal Corps Photograph, Library of Congress); background © 2011 Shutterstock

Manufactured in the United States of America

McFarland & Company, Inc., Publishers
  Box 611, Jefferson, North Carolina 28640
  www.mcfarlandpub.com

*I dedicate this book to my guerrilla friends
and to fellow officers who were lost during the
Japanese invasion of the Philippines and during
those horrible days in the Japanese prison camps.*

*I also include my wife, Mary,
and sons, Don and Charles,
who for years have put up with my idiosyncrasies,
many of which were rooted in those
years spent in the Philippines.*

Acknowledgments

I THANK Reyburn Myers for coping with my poor penmanship and misspelling; and for her literary help in getting this story together. Without her help this book would never have become a reality.

Thanks also to James Pope Simpson, a World War II veteran, and his wife, Annabeth, for reading the manuscript and offering encouragement and suggestions.

Foreword

THIS is the personal story of Col. Donald H. Wills for the time from April 6, 1942, when the Philippine Islands were invaded by the Japanese Imperial Forces, until April, 1945, when the islands were liberated by United States forces in the Far East under Gen. Douglas MacArthur.

The story is written from memory and notes made during that time and other recollections made later in 1945. More than 45 years have passed and there is the possibility that some dates or figures could be contested by other survivors of those times. It is possible that there are some errors, but they would be unimportant to the overall story.

All events really happened. There has been no attempt to slight the accomplishments of others who played important roles.

The bravery, suffering, and death of the defenders of the Philippines have been well documented. The courage and determination of forces retaking Leyte and Luzon have also been written about in some detail. Less well-known was the contribution of the American and Filipino guerrilla fighters who either escaped or refused to surrender and took to the hills to continue the struggle.

This is the story of one determined escapee, who, after experiencing cruelty, starvation, and hopelessness for two years in Japanese prison camps, realized that freedom was worth any risk. Alone he dared Japanese bullets, sharks, and the Pacific Ocean to reach Mindanao to fight on with the loyal Moros, Filipinos, and other Americans.

– D.H.W. and R.M.

Table of Contents

List of Maps and Illustrations

The Philippine Islands

THE Philippine Archipelago consists of about 7,000 islands strung in a line 800 to 1,000 miles long, covering 115,000 square miles between 5 and 17 degrees north of the equator, the same latitude as Central America. The northernmost islands are within 200 miles of Taiwan; the southernmost are within *vinta* travel to the Celebes. All the islands lie about 600 miles east of the China coast and fewer than half are larger than one square mile. Only eleven islands are large enough to be important to the economy of the nation. The largest island, Luzon, has 40,400 square miles, and the second largest, Mindanao, has 36,500 square miles. The population of the Philippines today is about 25 million people.

The climate is typical for the northern tropics: continuous heat with an average temperature of about 80 degrees, a high relative humidity, and abundant rainfall, averaging 50 to 150 inches a year. The dry and rainy seasons vary in different locales within the islands.

Probably the most interesting aspect of the islands is its people: a mixture of Chinese, Japanese, Indian, Spanish, Anglo-Saxon, and native Filipinos. The people can be traced to approximately four ethnic roots.

The Atas or Negritos, who are considered the aborigines of the Philippines, are found only in a few scattered elements in the interior mountains of parts of Luzon, Negros, and Mindanao.

The Indonesians or proto-malays are believed to have moved from the Asian highlands into the Philippines and Malaya via a land bridge about 8,000 B.C. Example of this ethnic strain are the Bontoc, Kalinga, Ilongots, Ifugao, and Igorots of the mountains of northern Luzon.

The third ethnic infusion into the islands was somewhat later and was composed of Malays from the islands to the south. Examples of this ethnic background are the Tagalogs, Cebuanos, and Ilocanos. Most of the people in the islands have this heritage.

The Moros (who follow Islam) entered the Philippine Islands about A.D. 1300 as tradesmen. They converted a number of those in the southern islands to Islam. They spread north as far as Luzon in the 15th and 16th centuries, but are now found only in the southern islands of Mindanao, Basilan, Palawan, Jolo, and the Sulu chain of small islands.

Politically the Philippines were under the domination of Spain until the

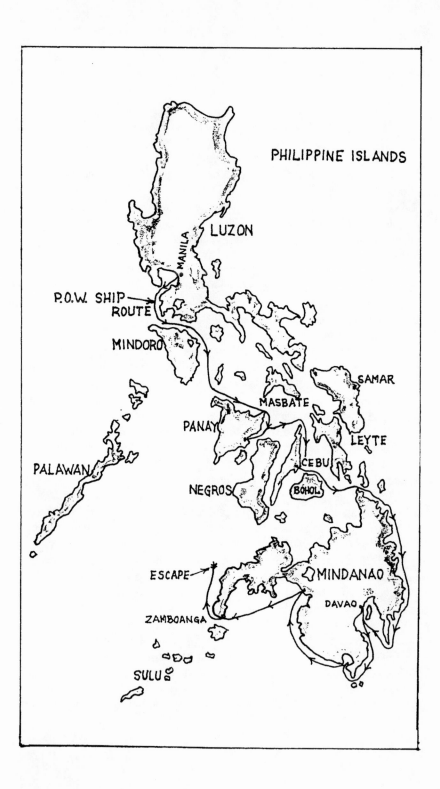

PHILIPPINE ISLANDS

LUZON

MANILA

P.O.W. SHIP
ROUTE

MINDORO

SAMAR

MASBATE

PANAY

LEYTE

CEBU

PALAWAN

NEGROS

BOHOL

ESCAPE

MINDANAO

DAVAO

ZAMBOANGA

SULU

American occupation in 1900. At the outbreak of World War II, they were a commonwealth under the United States. They received their independence July 4, 1946, under Pres. Elpidio Quirino. English and Spanish are spoken, but now the emphasis is on the national language of Tagalog. Other dialects are also spoken in various parts of the islands. English, however, is still the link between the various groups.

1. Escape

IN APRIL, 1944, rumors circulated throughout Davao Penal Colony Prison Camp in the Philippines that we were going to move. One story had us going to another camp; another had us being taken to Japan. I had already made up my mind that I was not going to Japan. I had come 700 miles farther south from Cabanatuan Prison Camp to be nearer our forces in the Southwest Pacific, and I sure was not going back. Time, however, was running out for my escape. In May we were advised that most of us would be moved. We would go by truck to Davao City, then by boat to Japan.

We were told June 1 that we would move the next morning. Much of the night we spent selecting what we could take and packing it. We could only take what we could carry and that would be limited to a couple of musette bags and a duffle bag. Over the last two years we had accumulated a lot of junk which would now have to be left behind. All of our homemade stoves, made from tin cans, and various bottles and pots had to be left in camp. Later that night, after packing, we decided to have a going-away feast. A couple of puppies were running around our barracks. I caught them, butchered them, and made a vegetable stew with comotes (a kind of yam), eggplant, and *kangkong* (a green plant which grew in ditches around the camp). The stew was really good, the puppies tasted a bit like veal or pork. Along with the last of our "tractor" alcohol, the meal was a great success. After all, the mountain tribes in Luzon eat dogs. We figured that we might as well enjoy them also. Buster Mills and I later recalled on many occasions what a good meal that was.

The next morning the first group of prisoners moved out at 5 A.M. The Japs had only 25 trucks so the move had to be made in two shifts. Naturally, with a name beginning with "W," I was in the second shift. The trucks were standard one-and-a-half ton army trucks and they put 30 of us in each truck. We got our instructions in comic English by a Mr. Wada, an interpreter. The second shift was loaded on the trucks at 12 noon. We were tied together by a rope around our waists, loaded on the truck with our bags, made to sit down, and blindfolded. We were required to remove our shoes, and as an extra precaution, we had to hold our hands in the air so the Jap guard at the front of the truck could see that we were not cutting the ropes. He had a long bamboo stick; if you lowered your hands, he let you have it on the head with the stick as a reminder. We also learned that there were Jap guards posted all along the road. There was no chance of escaping from the truck. In a couple of hours we arrived at the Lasang docks in Davao. The Japs took the blindfolds off and untied us. We were herded together and immediately loaded on barges, 100 men to a barge, and taken out to the boat, another old, American tramp steamer of about 2,500 tons. Several Jap naval vessels rode at anchor nearby in the harbor.

About 1,250 of us were put in the hold of the forward well deck. There were also about 1,000 Jap troops in the after well deck. We could use the deck space above us on a rotation basis. Jap guards with machine guns, rifles, and grenades watched us from positions around the deck. The ship pulled away from the dock, moved out into the bay, then moved over to a small island and dropped anchor. We remained there for several days. We had to sleep in shifts, one-third of the men would be sleeping while the other two-thirds stood and waited their turn. Food was rice and soup twice a day, brought up from the Jap kitchen at the other end of the ship. Water was limited and only cut on at certain times of the day. The weather was hot and we had the choice of roasting in the hold or baking on the deck.

When we finally moved out on June 11, we were leading a two-ship military convoy carrying Japanese troops and American POWs. Two gunboats and a Betty-type bomber escorted our two ships. We steamed down the Davao Gulf and at nightfall, we anchored in Saragani Bay on the south coast of Mindanao. The plane was still around and the gunboats patrolled our two-ship convoy. The Japs hung lights over the side of the ship. They took no chances on losing prisoners. I had thought of jumping over the side during the night, but the lights and the gunboats prevented that.

The next day we moved up the south coast of Mindanao and into Parang harbor. That night we also had floodlights and a patrol. The shore was so near yet so far! How inviting the green coconut trees, the white sand, and the nipa shacks looked. If only I could get to them! The next day we moved along the south coast of Mindanao to the Zamboanga Peninsula. We anchored in the stream off Zambo City.

We dropped anchor in the early evening. As many as could were on deck, sitting on the cargo booms, on the rail, and anywhere else they could find a seat. We had already had our afternoon meal, and we were enjoying the view of Zamboanga City off in the distance, about a mile away. The tropical night came on rapidly, lights began to blink from the city, and the cool of the evening felt good. We sat around on the cargo booms and deck machinery, dreaming of some way to get ashore.

As we dreamed we heard a splash and then rifle shots. The Japanese quickly herded us below deck and battened down the hatches. We stood in the dark and wondered what had happened. Word came down that someone had jumped overboard. The escapee was later identified as Lieutenant

Colonel McGee who had been stationed in Zamboanga City before and during the war. We hoped that he had made the swim ashore and found friends. (More on Colonel McGee later.)

As a result of the escape, we were confined below decks. The heat was stifling, and there was no place to sit down. With 1,250 men breathing, the oxygen gave out quickly. Men gasped for breath. The Japs had to partially open the hatch so we could get some air. It was a terrible night, I'm sure much like the infamous "black hole of Calcutta."

Early the next morning the Japs opened the hatches and asked for a detail to do some work on deck. The ship was underway, and we were moving up the west coast of Zamboanga. I was one of the volunteers to go topside. The Jap officer indicated that he wanted us to build a fence around the well deck using the six-foot-square, wooden life rafts. The Japs realized that they could not keep all of the 1,250 prisoners below deck and would have to let us rotate topside.

We pushed the life rafts up against the ship's rail to make a six-foot fence. However, because of the latrines built up on the railing, there were some spaces that the rafts would not fit into. The latrines were wooden cubicles built against the side of the ship and cleaned by hosing them down twice a day. There was one space on the port side between the latrine and a square water tank that the Jap lieutenant puzzled over. Finally, he had me pile some boxes in the space so no one could get near the rail. The Jap didn't notice, as I did, that the boxes formed nice steps right up to the top of the ship's rail. After we had finished the fence, no one was allowed to walk around on deck except to go to the latrine or when the water faucets were turned on.

After the fence-building work was finished, we workers were allowed to climb up on the cargo booms again and rest. It was early in the afternoon and we continued to move up the coast about three miles from shore. The green-clad mountains and the coconut palms on the coast seemed so close and yet far. I knew I must do something soon or I would end up in Japan. Any chance of an early end to prison camp would be gone. I knew that soon the ship would be swinging away from the coast and any swim to shore would be impossible. I estimated that by nightfall, we would be passing Coronado Point where the coast swings to the east. I would have to go before then. I went below to see Buster Mills, one of my close friends from camp, and we discussed the situation.

"Herb, I don't like the idea of jumping over the side. The guards will start shooting in a matter of seconds and everyone will be alerted to our escape. It seems to me it would be better to slip out one of the portholes."

"Buster, that's impossible. First, about a thousand guys will be watching us, and second, the porthole cover would have to be removed before you could even try to wiggle through the eighteen- or twenty-inch hole. I'm

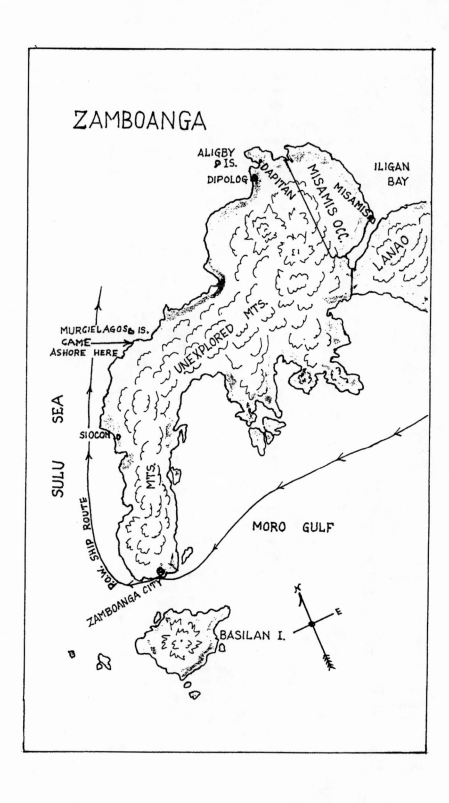

going over the side at dusk. It's now or never. I'll wait for about ten or fifteen minutes to give you time to go out the porthole, if you decide to, and I'll see you ashore."

I went back on deck, convinced that I would go alone. I began to analyze my chances. I had thoroughly thought out this escape. Although the Japanese guard was only about ten feet away from the spot where I was going over, I figured he could never reach me in time, once I got there without his expecting anything. A quick step up the boxes and to the rail and I would be gone.

First, I would go over the off-shore side of the boat. That way the Japs would think it was just a crazed prisoner committing suicide and wouldn't send the gun boats to look or delay the convoy. Second, I had heard that sharks (which are numerous in these waters) do not feed at night. Third, once I got into the water, I would swim around the stern of the boat and head for shore. The boat was making about nine knots, and I calculated that if I cleared the stern by about ten feet, I would not be sucked under by the screws. When I got closer to shore, I would be able to hear the surf which would guide me ashore. Once on shore, I would have enough medicine and knowledge of the jungle to exist for up to six months, or until I could contact friendly natives. I planned to be very careful whom I would contact. What I didn't know at the time was that the American camp commander, Colonel Olson, had assigned two Marine Corps sergeants to keep a watch on me to see that I didn't try to escape. Luckily, they failed in their jobs!

Back at my seat on the cargo boom, I began to consolidate by escape kit. I had a small Moro dagger which I had concealed among my meager possessions, and I had planned to knife the guard first and then dive over. But I ruled this out when I decided my chances would be better and things would be quicker if I didn't get involved with the guard. I remembered Charlie Harrison's disastrous attempt at the camp gate.

The 30-foot drop over the rail to the water would put me about amidship when I hit the surface. If I dived out as far as possible, I would be far enough away from the ship to avoid being sucked in by the screws as the stern went by. In my escape discussions, I had determined that if you clear amidship by ten feet, you should be safe from suction. We were traveling about eight or nine knots, and if I stayed under water as long as I could, the boat would be past when I came up. I wouldn't have to worry about small arms fire from either rifles or machine guns, because small arms fire only penetrates roughly 18 inches of water. If deeper than that, there is ample protection. I certainly planned to be deeper than 18 inches. I also figured that just for one man, they certainly wouldn't stop the ship or send back one of the corvettes. In the South China Sea, patrolled by U.S. submarines at that time, they certainly wouldn't turn on a searchlight as we were traveling in a blackout.

It seemed that I was taking a fairly good calculated risk. I didn't learn until later that sharks actually feed more actively at night, so I guess it was just pure luck that I wasn't bothered, because in this part of the Philippines, there are certainly plenty of sharks. As a matter of fact, coming by this same stretch of coast later on, I saw a number of sharks in the water and the Moros cautioned me about swimming.

When I came back up from the hold and climbed up to our platform on the cargo boom, most of the prisoners had covered themselves with pieces of canvas or cloth or whatever, and some were trying to get some sleep. I sat in my place and pulled up my piece of canvas. I opened my musette bag and took out some Red Cross food that I had saved. I decided to eat a decent meal right now. I didn't worry too much about the old belief about going swimming on a full stomach and getting stomach cramps. My meal consisted of a three-ounce can of ham and eggs, and one of my three chocolate bars. Previously, I had sealed these small chocolate bars in waterproof paper and kept them as an escape ration.

The man sitting next to me was eating a can of rations that he had saved, and we talked for a few minutes. The rain was coming down and he pulled up his piece of canvas and turned over to go to sleep after we finished eating. Just before dark, I had noticed that we were approaching some small rock islands, the Murcielagos Islands, lying a couple of miles offshore. The ship altered course slightly to pass outside these islands. At this point, the mainland of Zamboanga curved away to the east, and the ship was now gradually moving further and further away from the coast. Working fast was urgent as every minute I waited meant more hours that I would have to swim.

It began to rain harder. The Jap guards, at their places around the well deck and at the watertank, were bundled up in their raincoats and huddled against the superstructure. It was good and dark, and I was fairly certain that the guards couldn't see very well what I was going to do. As inconspicuously as possible, I pulled on an extra pair of socks, but left my shoes off. They certainly would be too heavy for swimming. I was wearing an old, one-piece coverall suit buttoned in front, an old tee shirt, and a pair of drawers the Japanese had given me. I had my army dogtags around my neck, and on a string around my waist, I had my VMI class ring and a small, gold lion's head ring that had come from my grandmother. I had kept them on this string for two years to keep the Japanese from getting them.

Working in the heavy rain and under the cover of darkness, I got my ID tag from my musette bag, my first lieutenant's bars, and a pair of crossed sabers. I put these in the breast pocket of the coveralls. I got two old Japanese socks and filled them with the medicine secured before we left Davao Penal Colony. I had a bottle of sulfathiozol tablets, about 500 grains – this was for dysentery – and some sulfanilamide tablets for infections. I also had a bottle of quinine tablets, roughly 750 grains. These, of course, were for malaria and were packed in an unbreakable tin container. There were two small bottles of atabrine, a total of 100 tablets, also for malaria. I had 100 multivitamin tablets, a syringe, and several vials of emetine for amoebic dysentery. I took my army prismatic compass that I had hidden for two years, my burning glass, the two remaining bars of chocolate, and as a last thought, I threw in a small bottle of sleeping pills, phenobarbital. I tied the two socks together, slipped them around my waist under my coveralls, and tied them securely.

The coveralls were baggy and loose, and the socks wouldn't be noticed. Although I was in good health and hadn't had malaria for several months, I only weighed about 125 pounds against my usual weight of 185. Perhaps being so thin and in comparatively good shape, having worked in the jungle for the past two years, enabled me to survive the coming long swim. I also took a small, round tin from my musette bag and slipped it into my pocket. It had been prepared back in Davao. Sealed inside was a small bottle of iodine, bichloride of mercury tablets for making sterile solutions, zinc oxide paste, some morphine, another hypodermic, a scalpel, a small pair of surgical scissors, a little bit of cotton, some gut sutures, and a needle. This was my escape kit. I had accumulated the contents a little at a time. I always figured that if I expected to survive in the jungle, I would need all the medicines I could carry.

The two chocolate bars would hold me until I could find some kind of food, always plentiful in the jungle. Also, there would be plenty of shellfish of all kinds along the seashore. In the small streams draining into the ocean, there would be fresh water shrimp and small fish. Certain leaves of trees are edible and at that time I could identify them. I could also eat certain roots and tubers that I had learned to recognize while at Davao Penal Colony. In retrospect, however, I made one mistake. I had no knife of any kind! I should have carried along the Moro dagger. Survival in the jungle is very difficult without a knife of some kind.

The rain was still coming down. Everyone around me seemed to be asleep. The man next to me, Capt. Charlie Brown, who had just come back from the latrine, and had a watch, told me it was eight o'clock. We talked in undertones for a few minutes, and then at what I thought was 8:15, I told him to cover up with my shelter and watch my bag for me as I was going to the latrine (benjo) and would be back in a few minutes. If he suspected anything, he never let on. As I climbed down from my perch on the boom, he was huddled under my shelter half.

It is hard to explain how I felt as I climbed down and approached the Japanese guard. I knew I was taking a big gamble, but strangely, any fear or apprehension was gone. For the moment at least, I wasn't thinking about whether or not I was going to make it. The decision had been made. It seems that in a situation like this, one has to concentrate on each second as it passes and make sure that everything goes right at that moment, according to the way it is planned. I was going through the whole plan by reflex, almost automatically.

I worked my way past the obstacles on deck and took a few steps toward the Jap guard. There was no fear, but I was so tense that my stomach was trembling and in a tight knot. When I stepped in front of him, the guard grunted questioningly. Every word of what I was going to say had been thought out: "Hatai watachi, benjo ka?" This was supposed to mean, "Mr. soldier, sir, may I go to the latrine?" I had meant to flatter him with the word, "sir." I didn't want to take any chances of having him try to stop me.

I slouched as much as I could to make it appear that I was tired and kind of sick. The rain came down and dripped off of the guard's helmet. He was huddled in his raincoat and looked as miserable as the night itself. He hesitated only a moment and then answered in a word that the Japs had picked up from us, "OK, OK," he said. I turned and took a few steps toward the latrine. I could feel him watching me in the dark, but I knew he couldn't see too well, and I knew he didn't notice the bulge of socks under my coveralls.

I reached the latrine and grabbed the two by four on the side and leaned against it for a minute. I wanted to act weak and a little sick. I glanced back to see if he was still watching me. He had turned and was looking at someone else coming to the latrine. Four feet away was the gap by the railing with the boxes piled up in front of it. I could see the wet, steel top of the railing. The four boxes presented a perfect step up the rail. I hesitated for just a moment, breathed a prayer, then with a wild heave on the two by four, I stepped up on the boxes ... one, two, three, four and onto the railing. I don't remember thinking about anything except getting up on that railing.

The guard screamed immediately. Out of the corner of my eye, I could see him lunge in my direction, his wet bayonet gleamed in the rain. He was too late. In that instant I plunged over the side. I tried to make a clean, deep dive, but it must not have been too good. I felt the water smack me in the face and tear at my loose coveralls. I don't know how far I went under, but it didn't seem very far. Almost immediately my air was gone and I clawed back to the surface. The coveralls seemed to hold me suspended in the water. When I reached the surface, a burst of machine gun fire churned the water by my head. I could feel the concussion of grenades exploding in the water. I got a mouthful of water. I could hear the smack of bullets. I took a half breath and dived again. Things happened so fast that I acted by instinct. When I came up again the stern of the ship was passing about ten yards away. I could hear yelling and shooting on deck and the dull explosions of grenades. The shots were not even close now. They must have lost me in the darkness. I was somewhat panicky and started to swim as fast as I could around the stern of the boat. I guess I wanted to get away from that shooting. Something caught in my coveralls and then tore loose. For a moment I thought it was a shark, but it must have been a wire (maybe the log wire) hanging over the stern. The coveralls made it very hard to swim, and I stopped a minute to catch my breath, telling myself to take it easy.

I looked up and out of the darkness loomed a big black hulk. With a start, I remembered the second boat in the convoy; it was bearing down on me. In spite of the waves and coveralls, I swam a crawl stroke as hard as I could. The boat passed about thirty feet away while I was still swimming. There was a flurry of shots, and I could hear the bullets smack the water close by.

I tried to get as far away as possible. Then, I realized my violent movement in the water was giving me away. My swimming had stirred up the phosphorescence, always present in tropical water, and I was leaving a telltale trail of silvery light with every movement. I stopped moving and sank with just my nose above the water. The waves kept slapping me in the face. Through the rain I could see the dim black outline of the second ship moving away. The shots weren't even close now.

Two red flares went up from the second boat, and I thought for a minute that they were going to send the corvettes back to look for me. Not daring to move, I floated until the flares had burned out. No boat came back.

The two transports faded into the darkness and I was alone. All shooting had stopped and the only sound was the hissing and lapping of the waves. I started to laugh. I laughed and laughed for several minutes at the top of my voice. I felt better, stronger. The fact that I was free, regardless of the position I was in, gave my morale a great boost. I felt better than I had for a long time.

A soft rain came down in the darkness. The water was not really rough, but it was choppy and a heavy sea was running. I knew I had a long swim ahead of me so I relaxed in the water as much as I could, trying to get my bearings. A couple of times I swallowed a mouthful of water. It was very salty. From the top of one of the waves I located the shore, a darker line against the dark sky. I knew there wasn't any hurry now, so I struck out, using an easy side stroke and changing sides every now and then so I wouldn't tire out any one set of muscles too fast. From time to time I would turn over and swim on my back, kicking my legs in a frog kick.

Later the coveralls began to get pretty heavy and seemed to be holding me back more and more. I decided to get rid of them. I must still have been pretty nervous because, just after I let the coveralls go, I remembered my can of medicine and the army papers in the pocket, but it was too late then. They were gone. However, I still had the two socks of medicine around my waist.

Later the rain stopped and there were a few stars visible in the clear patches in the sky. Once, on the top of a wave I looked ahead for the shore, as I had been doing from time to time to keep my bearings. This time all I could see was water. There was no land in sight. On the next wave I looked again . . . there was still no land. Then I happened to look over my shoulder and there was the land behind me. For some time I had been swimming back out to sea! This scared me so much it left me dry-mouthed and shaky. I had to figure out some way to keep in the right direction as I could not see the land all of the time while I was swimming. From the few stars that were visible, I picked out a group of two that would be over my left shoulder as I swam toward shore. From then on I kept those stars in sight over my left shoulder and I didn't have any more trouble.

I was tiring and I turned on my back to rest more and more often. Several times I got cramps in my legs but managed to work them out. I had gotten rid of everything except my underwear and the two socks of medicine now. I was determined to hang on to that medicine as I would certainly need it once I got ashore.

There were times when I was almost too tired to take a stroke. As it was, I was saving as much energy as I could and hardly lifted my arms out of the water when taking a stroke. More than once during these long hours I prayed. Later I began to hear a new noise, faintly at first, then steadier, stronger, nearer as the minutes went by. I could hear the rhythm of the breakers – I was getting closer to shore. Off to my left I could see the dark outline of the rocky Murcielagos Islands. They were much closer than the shore and I considered swimming to them. I decided that I would not be able to hide on the bare rocks and would still have to swim the next day, so I passed them up and kept on toward shore. The sky had cleared and the sea was now very smooth. I could see the outline of the land all of the time. There were several fires burning on shore.

Once, when an especially bad cramp hit my leg, panic struck. I yelled several times, hoping someone would hear me. Then, I thought the fires might be from a Jap outpost, so I kept quiet. Later, I learned the fires were made by Moro saltmakers, evaporating sea water. To be on the safe side, I steered clear of the fires and swam toward a dark spot on the beach.

Once, something brushed quite hard against my leg. Immediately, I thought of sharks. Something else nudged my leg. I kicked out as hard as I could, and that was all. Maybe it was just a piece of driftwood. Several times I ran into stinging nettles, and my face and shoulders burned like fire. Luckily, I didn't touch any deadly Portuguese men-of-war, which can kill with their sting.

As I got closer to land, I began to worry about where I was going to come ashore. I didn't want to land where the rock cliffs came down to the water as I might be injured by the waves dashing against the rocks. I picked out a spot on the horizon lower than that on each side of it, figuring that the higher profile would be closer to me and therefore a point of land. The space between would more probably be a beach of some kind. I also had the coral to worry about. With no shoes, I didn't want to cut my feet up and not be able to make a hike once I got ashore. As I got closer to the coast, I kept my body well up on the surface of the water and every now and then I reached down into the water at arms' length to see if I could touch bottom. In this way I intended to keep my feet off the coral.

The beach was very close now. The points of land were on each side and the sea was like glass. I kept swimming. Finally, my hand touched sand on the bottom. I found myself in about two and a half feet of water. I was lucky. There was no coral to walk over. I had come in on a small sand beach, about 100 yards long, between two rocky points of land.

The night was bright and clear. From the position of the stars, I figured it must be about 1 or 2 a.m. I had been in the water three or four or maybe five hours. It seemed a lot longer. Later, in calculating where I escaped from the boat on the offshore side of the rocky Murcielagos (bat) Islands, I figured I had been four miles offshore.

I lay in the shallow water resting for a while. Then I tried to stand up. My legs gave way and I fell down again. My legs were too weak to hold me up. I had been in the water too long. I crawled up on shore and lay resting in the sand for some time, but I began to feel cold. I was freezing. Even though body temperature is 98 degrees, the water temperature must have been around 75 to 80. Having been in the water so long, my body temperature was certainly somewhat lower than the normal 98 degrees, thus I felt very cold.

I finally was able to get up. I walked up and down the beach, stimulating the circulation in my legs. Then I jogged a while to get warm. Then I looked around for a spot to sleep.

There was a pile of rocks a little way back from the water. I scooped out a place in the sand by these and tried to sleep. The mosquitoes were terrible. I tried covering up with sand which helped all except my face. I little later some wild carabao, or wild tamaro, came down to the beach and started snorting and nosing around. To be on the safe side, I climbed on top of the rockpile to finish out the night. The mosquitoes were so bad that I decided to take some sleeping pills to get as much rest as possible before dawn when I would probably have quite a bit of hiking to do. I got the bottle of sleeping pills (phenobarbitol) out of one of my socks and swallowed two of the pills. I waited for about fifteen minutes and nothing happened, so I took two more pills. Still nothing happened. So I took two more.

The next thing I knew it was morning and the sun was shining in my face. I was startled. I had slept well into the day and could have been found by anyone coming down to the beach. I quickly climbed down off the pile of rocks. There was no one in sight. I crawled into the bushes in back of the beach to hide and take in my surroundings. The mosquitoes had really eaten on me during the night. I had red spots all over me. I could see my arms and legs and could imagine that my face looked like I had a case of measles.

Those black mosquitoes found on the beaches and near the streams are smaller than the regular ones, but their bite is really terrible. They are so small that they can get through ordinary mosquito netting. The Filipinos call them nit-nits.

Besides the mosquito bites and the red rash from the stinging nettles, I was none the worse for my swim. My hearing did seem a little dull and my ears ached. This condition lasted for about three days.

I did have a cut on my left wrist about an inch long and half an inch deep. I could only guess it was from a fragment of one of the many grenades thrown into the water when I dived overboard. It had gone unnoticed in the confusion. Washed clean by the sea, the small wound was puckered and white. I crushed up a sulfa pill with two beach pebbles and packed the cut full. I now took an inventory of my belongings; one underwear shirt, a pair of white cotton underwear shorts, my army dog tags on a string around my neck, and on a string around my waist the VMI class ring and the lion's head ring. I was wearing two pairs of socks and in two socks tied around my waist I had my remaining stock of medicine: 100 sulfathiazol tablets, a small bottle of sulfanilamide, a can of quinine tablets, two small bottles of atabrine, a bottle of multivitamins, the bottle of sleeping tablets, a small bottle of bichloride of mercury tablets, my army prismatic compass, a burning glass, and two small tropical chocolate bars from the Red Cross package. All of the other medicines in two cans in the pockets of my coveralls had been lost when I jettisoned the coveralls during the long swim to shore.

With these meager belongings I now had to survive long enough to contact friendly guerrillas. The thought of failure never entered my mind. Having been lucky enough to escape and get ashore safely, I now planned to clear the next hurdle: find friendly natives.

The little beach I had landed on was about one hundred yards long and a fairly uniform thirty or forty feet wide, between two rocky points of land which were covered with thick bushes. Behind the beach the land rose gradually to a height of several hundred feet. Large jungle trees covered the hills. Open patches of cogon grass on the hills on each side of the beach, however, enabled me to see how the land rose. A small stream flowed into the ocean at one end of the beach. Offshore, at some distance, I could see the rocky, uninhabited Murcielagos Islands that our ship had passed shortly after I jumped overboard.

It was at this time that my thoughts went back, and I drifted off into memories of the past horrible 26 months which began on that day in April 1942 on the Bataan Peninsula.

2. Surrender and Prison

THE battle for Luzon had gone badly for the United States forces in the Philippines (USFIP) at Lingayan Gulf, and my unit, the 26th Cavalry of the Philippine Scouts, had been assigned the difficult duty of conducting the rear-guard defense of all the North Luzon forces as they retreated into the Bataan Peninsula.

Over the weeks conditions in Bataan, sickness and starvation, had reduced our forces to a pitifully inadequate defense against the fresh Japanese troops brought in from Malaya to make the final assault on Bataan. Our forces, made up mostly of Philippine army units, were in the final stages of trying to stop the Japanese from overrunning our front lines.

Bataan changed my attitude toward butterflies and my understanding of "freedom." I had always connected butterflies with beauty and life, and I didn't fully appreciate freedom until I lost it. But all that came later.

That day in April, 1942, Sergeant Torio and I were worried about the advancing Japanese troops, and how to get our own men of the 26th Philippine Scouts down the west coast and up the east coast of Bataan Peninsula. The Japanese army had pushed out of northern and then southern Luzon into the Bataan Peninsula where they were threatening our positions.

"Sergeant Torio, I suppose we're not the only cavalry outfit that has eaten their horses instead of riding them." He laughed in a grim way. "Lieutenant Wills, I wish I had those horses to get down these roads." He looked up the winding, narrow trail, a foot deep in dust, which twisted through the thick forest rising on either side. The dust barely concealed the potholes which would not have bothered our recently forfeited cavalry horses.

"Sergeant, be glad it's the dry season or we'd have a foot of mud," I pointed out, trying to cheer him up.

"Lieutenant, how can we get the troops around the end of Bataan and up the east coast in those buses?" He motioned toward the row of elderly vehicles drawn up beneath trees on each side of the trail. The "Manila" letters that indicated they were city cast-offs had faded to a shadow. The dents and chipped paint, visible even in the dusk and dust, indicated the age and condition of the transportation, brought from Manila to Bataan. This was our transportation since the horses had been turned in, subsequently butchered, and issued as rations to all the troops on Bataan.

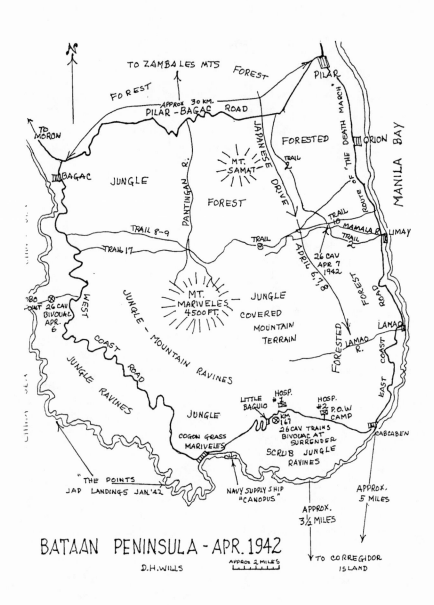

This map of the Bataan Peninsula shows the coast road, trails, and some troop details as of April 6–9, 1942, at the time of the American surrender.

By this time the thousands of people on Bataan had exhausted the food supply. We shot monkeys, wild pigs, and collected edible leaves to supplement the small amount of rice available for each person.

"Orders are orders, Sergeant, so we'll do it. This isn't a regimental motor officer's dream, especially not a cavalry outfit, but it's better than walking. The Japanese have broken through the Mt. Samat position and we're supposed to provide delaying action along the Mamala River and help out General Bluemel and the 31st Infantry, an American outfit, the only one on Bataan. Our orders are to move over there tonight and be on hand at dawn at the junction of Trails 2 and 10. You know the terrain better than anyone, Sergeant, so you'll lead the troop movement. I'll bring up the rear with the two repair trucks, the Bren guns, and the old Hudson sedan that came with the buses. By the way, start praying that those Bren carriers don't throw a track every time we make a sharp turn or hit a pothole."

Sergeant Torio, a neat, career Filipino Scout, assisted me in my role as regimental transportation officer. A Tagalog from central Luzon, he was probably about 33. He was a willing, good-humored asset. His determined approach to our grim situation proved to be a real morale builder for me.

Sergeant Torio forced a smile as he hurried off. He did look glummer than I had ever seen him. The troops with their gear were already boarding the buses. I had to get ready to move out. If you've never struggled with a Bren carrier, you can't understand what we were up against. The carriers move on tracks just like a tank. When you want to turn, you push a lever which locks the left track so that the carrier pivots left, or you lock the right lever and the carrier pivots to the right. This works OK unless you hit a rock or turn too fast and throw a track. Then the crew spends half an hour jacking up, uncoupling the track, and putting it back on. We carried emergency equipment: jacks, lug-wrenches, saws, and shovels. But the men were doing these repairs by flashlight, in a foot of dust, with mosquitoes and the pressure to hurry. Everyone knew we were needed up front to try to stave off disaster.

We traveled down Trail 9, blacked out and sharing the trail with other Philippine army units. When we hit the main road, "bang" went the first Bren carrier. After much swearing and sweating, the men got the track back on and we moved out briskly, traveling all night with lights out along the coast highway which was a graded, two-lane, dirt road. At dawn on April 17 we arrived at Trails 10 and 2, two miles from Limay and near the Mamala River. On high ground we could see Manila Bay.

The trails had been cleared by the army engineers. The narrow, two-way unsurfaced roads allowed two vehicles to pass each other carefully. The trails theoretically permitted troop movements around the interior of Bataan under the cover of jungle trees rather than the exposed passage on the main road around Bataan one or two kilometers from the coast.

Each time we camped, soldiers used bolos and cleared undergrowth at the edge of the trail. They backed vehicles into these clearings and set up mess tents. The buses were sent back south to the motor pool and our train, made up of supply trucks, maintenance trucks, scout cars, and Bren guns, was ordered to bivouac in the clearings in the jungle.

Sergeant Torio and I discussed the situation and I talked to some of the troops out of the 31st Infantry coming down from the north on Trail 2. They were exhausted and apprehensive and reported that the Japanese had broken through and were advancing south rapidly.

Sergeant Torio and I decided to go up Trail 2 to get the facts and, if possible, to find our headquarters and get orders as to what to do with the trains. We fired up the old camouflaged Hudson that had come from Manila with the buses, and started northward.

Up the trail we soon discovered bombed and burning vehicles of every kind which blocked the road. Passage was impossible. Huge craters could swallow a car. Flames crackled through much of the underbrush. We didn't wait for another warning. Sergeant Torio pulled the Hudson into a grove of trees well off the trail. We continued up the trail on foot, staying along the edge in the shelter of the towering trees.

In the clogged trail, vehicles jammed bumper-to-bumper had become burned-out skeletons. A scout car teetered perilously on the edge of a huge crater, its machine gun ammunition belts hung from the receiver, the gun pointing aimlessly at nothing. Everywhere we saw devastation and waste. We saw few bodies. At least most of the troops had escaped and were alive somewhere in the jungle.

"Lieutenant Wills, where's the American Air Corps?" Sergeant Torio asked. "We can't do much when the Japanese control the air."

"We keep hearing rumors that help is on the way, that aircraft carriers will arrive and pull us out of this mess. But remember, Sergeant, it's just a rumor." Such rumors had been around so long, we didn't believe them anymore.

As we proceeded cautiously around a bend, we came on a bombed-out and burning ordnance truck. A Filipino sergeant lay beside the trail, one leg of his uniform soaked in blood. We went over to him. Sergeant Torio started to offer his canteen, but the wounded sergeant pointed to his own canteen lying beside him.

"Can we help you, soldier?" Sergeant Torio knelt and put his hand on the man's forehead, testing for fever.

"Bad hit in the leg, sir. I can't walk. I think it's a compound fracture from shrapnel."

"Lieutenant Wills, this man should be moved into the shade and under cover. Do you think we can move him safely?" Sergeant Torio looked anxiously at the sky. No Jap plane had been over for some time. We knew one was due. Since daylight the Japs had patrolled the roads looking for targets.

"I guess you'd better move yourselves." The wounded sergeant tried to grin. "The Japs are making bombing and strafing runs all the time. They'll be back before long."

"Sergeant Torio, we can't leave him here." I turned to the wounded man. "Sergeant, we've got to move you. Can you stand it?"

We had no blanket or anything we could use as a stretcher, so Sergeant Torio took his head and shoulders, and I took one leg and used his pants to support the wounded leg and keep it straight. Keeping him near the ground, we eased him back into the jungle, well away from the edge of the trail. The sergeant's mouth and face were rigid with pain, but he seemed glad to be away from the sun and dust and beneath the shelter and shade of densely clustered mango trees and on the far side of another truck as yet virtually undamaged.

"The Japs aren't stupid," he said. "Now that they've bombed the vehicles and clogged the roads, where would the men be? Along the edge of the trails in the jungle, so they bomb and strafe along the edges. Could you help me find my unit or maybe help my unit find me? I'm with the 57th Infantry."

"We'll try when we move up the trail. If we find some of your outfit, we'll tell them where you're hidden. Sergeant Torio, check his canteen. Does he have enough water?"

"It's OK—within reach and nearly full, Lieutenant." He turned to the wounded Scout. "I'm sorry we can't take you along. You're not bleeding now. This is about all we can do for you and about the best place we can find to leave you."

As we moved on up the trail, we approached a riverbed which at this season was dry. We were making our way down the bank when we heard, growing louder, the not-too-distant hum of a plane. Instantly Sergeant Torio and I dropped down behind a huge, half-rotten old stump on the low side of the riverbank. A Japanese Nakajima fighter flew down the trail, so low we could see the pilot, in his brown leather helmet and goggles, looking down over the side of the cockpit. The bomb fell on the other side of the stump; the stump disintegrated in a blinding flash, covering us with rotting wood and sawdust.

We were lucky. The stump broke the force of the explosion and shielded us from shrapnel. A Filipino soldier who was making his way toward the river near the stump didn't make it. He lay beside the road in a pool of blood.

Several men broke out of the underbrush along the trail after crossing the riverbed. No one stayed in the open any longer than absolutely necessary. The men reported that they had orders to head south.

"Sergeant Torio, we'd better head south with the rest of them and try to find out what we're supposed to do." We brushed the sawdust from each other and started back. We headed deeper into the jungle each time we heard the drone of a plane.

"I've hunted deer and rabbits back in Virginia, Sergeant. Now I know how they felt."

When we reached the Hudson, still safely hidden, we realized that we couldn't drive down the clogged trails, so we headed the Hudson down an embankment into the dry Mamala riverbed. Captain Burgess from the 26th and three Filipino Scouts joined us. We six put quite a strain on the old Hudson, commandeered out of Manila for use as a staff car on Bataan. A 1937 model, it had already seen a rough life. A sedan, now painted an olive drab and camouflaged with smears of mud, it actually ran pretty well and had been one of our better staff cars.

For the trip out, with Sergeant Torio driving, we all pushed, shoved, and lifted the old car into the dry streambed. Since it was the dry season, there was a wide expanse of sand, sometimes soft and deep, and a few boulders scattered here and there.

Everyone piled in and with all windows open and a sharp watch for bombers, we started down the dry riverbed. We made good time in second and low gear, dodging around the boulders, bumping along and trying to pick out the hardest sand. The bottom of the car constantly dragged on the sand. Once in a while the wheels would sink down and start to spin. We all piled out and shoved the old car onto more solid streambed, meanwhile listening and watching the sky.

Luckily no bombers came over. I guess the Japanese figured they had already wrecked everything on the road and so they didn't think it necessary or else we were just lucky.

Actually we covered the approximately three miles in about 30 minutes, but it seemed longer with our fear of bombers and getting permanently stuck. When we came to the main highway, everyone, except Sergeant Torio, the driver, piled out again and shoved the old car up the bank and onto the road. The old Hudson was still running smoothly after plowing through all that sand and bumping over rough terrain. I felt a kind of affection for the old car. Back on the road and inside again, we headed down toward our bivouac.

On the morning of April 8, we learned that we were to bivouac at highway marker 167 and prepare to surrender at dawn on the following morning. We were near Cabcaben. What was left of the trains were parked under trees. Soldiers slept in the open. The men had mixed feelings. Surrender? The word wasn't in our vocabularies. Another order came through. All officers were to surrender with their troops or face court-martial after the war.

"Sergeant Torio, they won't make that stick. There's plenty of jungle out here. We could make it back up to northern Luzon and exist there a long time, maybe with the Negritos in the Zambales Mountains."

By late evening it became obvious that I wouldn't have a choice. I was running a fever, shaking with chills, and feeling really lousy. Up to this time I had gotten 9 hours' sleep out of the last 110. Sergeant Torio helped me over to a Filipino doctor who was assigned to our regiment. He diagnosed my ailment as "febrile influenza." When Colonel Vance, the CO, came by, he took one look at me and ordered Sergeant Torio to take me to the hospital.

"Take my car, Sergeant, and then come back here. Lieutenant Wills is too sick. He should be in bed. We don't know what is going to happen around here in the next couple of days."

Sergeant Torio helped me into the sedan and drove up the main road to Hospital No. 2. This hospital consisted of a number of army tents scattered in the jungle about 500 yards off the main road. Some tents were for surgery and some for intensive care. Less serious cases had cots with mosquito nets under the trees. This was one of only two hospitals on Bataan.

I hated to say goodbye to Sergeant Torio. We had been through a lot together. We shook hands, and with a sinking feeling, I watched the sedan disappear in the dust. I was sick and losing touch with my outfit, the 26th Cavalry. That was the last time I saw Sergeant Torio.

An American corpsman hustled me into bed under the trees. He examined me and pronounced my illness malaria. He started me on a course of quinine. I didn't know much of anything for the next two or three days. During periods of clearheadedness I felt desperate. I was alone, in strange surroundings, and with an uncertain future or no future at all.

The hospital still sheltered about 2,000 patients, Filipino and American. Most of the American staff of doctors and all of the American nurses had been taken to Corregidor in Manila Bay. Left to tend the patients were a couple of doctors, a few American corpsmen, and some civilians.

The first few days after the Bataan surrender, nothing much happened at the hospital. When I finally became aware of things around me, there were Jap guards at the entrances to the hospital. Other than that, we were left alone. The troops on Bataan had been ordered to congregate at Little Baguio, Cabcaben, and Mariveles, and were being marched out of Bataan in groups of 1,000. In the hospital we could hear the movement of the prisoners along the road, but we weren't to know the awful story of the "Death March" until later.

We sick and wounded were cared for by corpsmen and able-bodied patients well enough to help out. After the prisoners had marched out of Bataan, the Japanese busied themselves with erecting a barbed wire fence around the hospital. All of this time the Japs were moving in their artillery. These guns ultimately ringed the hospital. We learned that the Japanese brought in 600 pieces, all pointed toward the bay. The first one of the incessant barrages that were to follow day and night showed us the target – Corregidor.

The defenders fired back with naval guns, targeting the points of fire and, thus, the hospital. We soon became aware of an odd fact. These shells travel faster than the speed of sound, so we heard the shells burst near us before we heard the booms of the naval guns that fired them!

I doubt that the gunners on Corregidor even knew that the hospital was in their impact area. I'm sure they tried to keep shells away from any hospital area, but in several cases shells ripped into the wards. One shell killed 8 men and wounded 21. Shrapnel whistled through the trees and dropped, burning hot, on patients and their cots.

The ten-inch mortar shells made a freight-train sound as they were lobbed in. When these hit the ground and exploded, they left craters as big as a house. We hated to hear them coming in. There was nothing we could do. We were helpless and could only hope that one of the mortar shells didn't hit close by. I now knew how the soldiers in World War I felt under an artillery barrage. At least they had dug-outs and shelters to get in. We had nothing and never knew, during that month of artillery dueling between the Japanese and Corregidor defenders, when the hits would impact the hospital area.

The bombardment went on night and day until Corregidor fell on May 6. "Bed rest" at the hospital became a grim joke. After the Corregidor surrender, the Japanese gave us more attention. The guards under a Sergeant Ocinono began to carry out orders. On the second day after Corregidor fell, the Filipinos were told that they could leave. About 700 limped, hobbled, or tottered out of Hospital No. 2. Many left with fever, with compound fractures, with gangrene. They should not have gone, but they were anxious to be away from the Japanese. Many must have died on the way home.

As soon as the Filipinos were gone, all bed patients were evacuated to Hospital No. 1. About 700 were left including one woman. No one knew why she was there except that she had a small baby about two weeks old. The woman had cut her hair and wore a man's khaki shirt and pants. The Jap guards discovered her. Six or seven shoved her with the rifle butts toward the jungle. She held her baby tightly, screaming in protest. I and several other Americans confronted the guards, but they lowered their bayonets and threatened us. The group continued on into the jungle, the guards herding the protesting woman. We did not see her again. We complained to a higher officer who issued orders that this would not happen again. But it was too late for that unfortunate woman. Sergeant Ocinono explained with a smile that "Soldiers will be soldiers."

Recovered from malaria, I began to think about how to survive as a prisoner of war. Some instinct told me to hide anything of value, so I put my Virginia Military Institute ring, the gold lion's head ring from my grandmother, and a compass on a string and tied them around my waist. My hunch paid off. The next day Jap troops came through the hospital, taking watches, jewelry, coins, anything of value. The soldiers did not search us or look in our pockets. They simply pointed at a ring or watch and motioned that the item should be given to them. No one argued with soldiers with bayonets and rifles on their backs. My small store of valuables remained around my waist.

The Japanese didn't spend much feeding us. We were given a bowl of red rice once a day with gravy made from rice flour toasted to make it brown. Twice we got some dried fish and once some carabao meat. The rations were given to the American kitchen detail. They prepared the food in large cooking pots called *kawas*. The patients filed by with messkits, if they had them, or cans if they did not, for their share.

The rice ration was never enough, so, under guard, we went into the jungle and foraged. We caught lizards and birds, picked fruit, nuts, green leaves and bamboo shoots, and dug camotes (a kind of sweet potato) – anything with some promise of nutrition. Once in a while a Jap guard would shoot a wild pig and give us part of the meat. We also found caches of GI rations and medicines which had been hastily discarded before the surrender.

I teamed up with three lieutenants, Young, Gates, and Holmes. They were Americans who had been serving with the Philippine army or the 31st Infantry and had also been in the hospital with malaria or dysentery and were now recovered. We scoured the area around the hospital. Seventy thousand troops on Bataan, 60,000 Filipino and 12,000 American, had marched out of the peninsula leaving everything they had. The approximately 25,000 Filipino civilians who had fled the Japanese to Bataan had evaporated by hiding in the jungle or had walked out with the hospital patients.

We found one large supply of medicine abandoned by some medical unit. It included quinine, atabrine, bismuth subcarbonate, paregoric, topical anesthetics, bandages, and painkillers. We found every conceivable kind of medicine or medical equipment. A chemistry major and pre-med student in college, I understood the value of these medicines. We filled a footlocker with them. Somewhere and somehow I knew our lives would depend on these medicines.

We became hardened to death. In the hospital Filipinos with stinking compound fractures had died from lockjaw and gangrene, others from malaria and dysentery. On the trails we found bodies so flattened by traffic and so dried by heat, dust, and sun, that they resembled pieces of leather and not human bodies. We peered into bombed vehicles and found reeking corpses. Everywhere on Bataan there was wrecked equipment and the bodies of unburied soldiers which resembled an untidy bundle of clothes, stained brown by the rotting flesh.

Once on a food detail we stumbled on a grove of cashew trees. Lieutenant Gates, a huge ordnance man from Tennessee, could never get enough food for his big body. He loved cashew nuts. Cashew trees grow a fruit somewhat like an apple with a pod on the bottom which contains the nut. Tennessee is pretty short on cashew trees, so unknowing Lieutenant Gates pried into the pods to break out the nuts. The finger-like growths exude an oil with the same characteristics and effects as our poison ivy and poison oak. Poor Gates enjoyed the rich nuts after toasting them, but by night, a rash covered his arms and cheeks, and his eyes were tiny slits in this swollen face. He had to put up with this for about a week.

Late one afternoon we came upon a mound of butterflies on the trail. A ray of sunlight through the trees turned their wings into vivid blue and yellow shimmering loveliness. As we approached, they rose in a cloud and drifted off, exposing a corpse. These symbols of beauty had been feeding on the body fluids of a dead soldier. This event changed my attitude toward butterflies, permanently. When I see them now I always think of that day in Bataan and of the death and destruction and rotting bodies.

We existed from day to day, concentrating on surviving. A number of times we saw monitor lizards feeding on bodies. Several times we ate monitor lizard tails, and we couldn't help but think that this was a sort of cannibalism once removed. But the lizard meat was not bad, something like a cross between chicken and frog legs.

From the stirring around the hospital and the increasing activity among the Japanese, we knew something was about to happen. Word filtered down. On May 25 we were being moved to Manila. Under Japanese direction we moved the hospital equipment out to the main road, supposedly to be picked up by Jap trucks at a later time.

On the morning of May 25 a convoy of Japanese army trucks arrived. We loaded 30 men and their gear to a truck and moved off for San Fernando, Pampanga, but not before we had to move the hospital equipment back to the hospital. Not enough trucks! Lt. Young, from a tank battalion, helped me load the footlocker of medicine. The 80-mile trip took all day. We stood in the truck beds. In the evening we pulled into a schoolyard. It was dirty, open-aired, fenced-in, and with no facilities. This yard had been used by the Bataan death marchers and the filth left by their stopover was still there. We had one meal of cold rice balls. Some of the men had dysentery and could barely walk. One corner of the yard served as a latrine. The lone water faucet ran at a trickle. The Japanese continued their brutality. Many men were beaten with sticks when they couldn't move fast enough. One soldier was downed with a rifle butt. Pleas for more water and food went unanswered. The Japanese had no compassion. Our sorry plight didn't seem to bother them in the least. We were treated like animals that didn't deserve any more sympathy than they would give to a cur dog.

When we were to resume the trip the next morning, we were told that only personal items that could be carried would be allowed on the trucks. Young and I had to open the footlocker and divide up the medicines. I filled my corpsman's bag as full as I could get it with the supplies I knew I would need. Lieutenant Young took as much as he could pack. We found some prisoners who were doctors. They took all the supplies they could cram into their personal bags. We finally got it all distributed and left the footlocker in the schoolyard.

At dawn after a miserable night on the filthy ground, we loaded onto the trucks and rumbled into Manila and downtown to grim old Bilibid prison. The ground for a bed even in a filthy schoolyard seemed luxurious when compared to Bilibid. Here we slept on concrete floors, no pillow, no pad, no nothing, but at least the floor was fairly clean. The POWs from Corregidor were also brought into Bilibid at this time.

As the prisoners from Corregidor marched in through the big iron gates of Bilibid, we stared in amazement. In spite of the fact that most of them had been forced to sit out in the sun for several days on bare concrete, their appearance was a shock to us. They looked fit and well fed. There had been more food on Corregidor even up to the end. While they were lucky enough to have some regular army rations, we on Bataan had been existing on a meager rice issue, supplemented with whatever we could glean out of the jungle. In addition, the men on Bataan had been exposed to malaria and dysentery to a much greater extent and it showed in our emaciated bodies and haggard faces.

We stayed in Bilibid only three days. By May 29 when we were to move out, I was sick again. I was nauseated, running a high fever, and jaundiced. There was only one disease that these symptoms indicated: hepatitis. I had picked it up in Hospital No. 2 somehow. I wanted desperately to stay with my group. When survival is at issue, you want to know the people you're with. I dug into my corpsman's bag and dosed myself with aspirin and nembutal, paregoric, and bismuth subcarbonate. This relieved the pain and diarrhea and the nausea sufficiently for me to leave with my group for the march to the train station. We trudged through the streets of Manila with the Filipinos silently watching us from the sidewalks.

At the station we loaded into narrow-gauge boxcars ($40' \times 8'$) sardine fashion, 90 to 100 men per car. We could not sit down, there was not enough room, so most stood, crammed together with a Jap guard at each door. I managed to get a place by a door. As the day wore on and the heat inside the car became intense, I could at least get a breath of air. From time to time we would rotate and let some of the other prisoners get a chance at some fresh air.

After three hours we stopped at a small depot at San Fernando. The prisoners were allowed to buy food from the Filipino women, boys, and old

Bilibid Prison
Manila, P. I.
1865-1945

men who were hawking their wares along the tracks. No young Filipino men were in sight. Philippine delicacies *balut, bud-bud* (coconut candies wrapped in banana leaves), and *bibinka* (puffed up sweet rolls), peanut candy, and a few fruits were offered for sale. *Balut* is a boiled incubated duck egg. Highly prized by the Filipinos, this appetizer would not appeal to the ordinary American, but hungry POWs ate practically anything. The bananas, star apples, and fried chicken pieces looked good to us, especially if we had the money to buy them.

The train started north again. In the late afternoon we arrived at the town of Cabanatuan. When I saw trucks gathered at the depot, I felt a great surge of relief. I assumed the trucks would carry us to the prison camp. I was not certain that I could walk the 20 kilometers to camp since the heat, crowding, hepatitis, and lack of food had left me shaky and weak in the knees. But such luxury was not to be. The men who could not stand up received transport. The Jap guards deemd me able to walk. So I started out. After the next five miles, I could not go on. I lay down beside the road and gave up. By that time it made no difference to me whether I was left to die or killed on the spot.

The guard hustled me off the road into a kind of schoolyard. Japanese soldiers were evidently living there in a nipa hut. My guard told me to lie in the yard and a truck would come back later to pick up stragglers. I could then ride it into camp.

The Japanese soldiers took no interest in my presence. I never figured out what they were doing nor did I care. I guess they were camped there waiting for transfer somewhere else. In due course, as promised, the truck chugged up the road and stopped at the schoolhouse yard. I climbed into the truck along with my precious corpsman bag and duffle bag. I cannot figure to this day why the soldiers didn't go through my bag while I lay in the yard. If they had, I would have lost everything that helped to keep me alive in the days and weeks to come.

Opposite: **This view of the main gate to Bilibid Prison in Manila, reveals the forbidding appearance of the old fortress. I spent time here on two different occasions. The Japanese used this as a gathering point when they were shifting prisoners to various locations.**

3. Cabanatuan Prison Camp

ON THE night of May 30, I arrived at the infamous Cabanatuan prison camp. We stayed one night and then moved six kilometers back toward town to Cabanatuan Camp No. 1. Luckily when we arrived, the Japanese did not inspect our baggage. We were told by other prisoners that, before, they had inspected all equipment and confiscated any medicine or food that the prisoners had, saying that it would not be needed!

The camp had been a Filipino army cantonment. The barracks, built of bamboo, were about 75 feet long, on stilts about two feet off the ground, with split bamboo floors, *sawali* sides, and nipa palm-leaf roofs. *Sawali* consists of flattened bamboo slats woven in panels which could swing up to let in air. We had an 18-inch walkway down the center of the barracks which left a sleeping platform six feet in depth on each side. The bunks were in two tiers, the top tier about four and one-half feet above the lower. I found a lower bunk and stowed my meager possessions in my alloted 24-inch-wide space. The Japanese divided us into three groups. In time we would number altogether about 6,000 men. Now we were much less than that.

In the next few days the Japanese commander, Colonel Mori, appointed the American camp commander and he selected his staff and assistants to administer the camp. Rosters were made up, barrack chiefs appointed, kitchen details made up. Cook areas and first-aid areas were designated. The latrines, open slit trench types, were established at the rear of the rows of barracks, back against the camp wire fence. There were only three water taps in our whole area and access to these was set up on a rotation basis as they were only turned on for a limited time during the day. There was no set schedule when the Japanese would turn on the water, so we had to keep a lookout. When the tap was turned on, a long line quickly formed. We never knew how long the water would be on.

In the next few weeks the camp became an operating unit. Across the road from the barracks, the hospital area was also established. The main function here was to bury the corpses each day as there was practically no medicine or equipment available.

Early in June, 1942, Americans were brought in from Camp O'Donnell so our ranks grew in number and the barracks were filled. As the prisoners from O'Donnell arrived, some in trucks and some marching, we lined up by the fence to inspect the newcomers. Again we watched in shock, but this time the men looked even worse than we did. The conditions at O'Donnell, in addition to causing the deaths of thousands, as we learned later, had reduced the survivors to walking skeletons. It was almost painful to watch them as they lined up for a head count, carrying their meager belongings in bags or sacks or rolled up in bundles. I had never seen a more pitiful looking bunch of men.

Now that our camp was at its 6,000-men capacity, we waited in line for hours at one of the three water taps. Many times as we approached our goal, the water was turned off and we were left thirsty and standing at a dry faucet.

Life in camp was a continual battle for survival. The men became walking skeletons on our food ration, about 10 ounces (a large sardine can scoop) of *lugow*, a watery rice, and *kangkong*, a plant which grew in the ditches around the camp. We collected this plant, and boiled it into soup. The resulting concoction resembled spinach or potato leaves floating in green water. Now and then the Japanese would kill a carabao. They took the meat and gave us what we called the NRA issue: neck, ribs, and anus. We cooked this up into a greyish stew which was divided among the 2,000 men in our area.

The death toll in camp mounted to 30 or 40 a day from scurvy, pellagra, malnutrition, and unidentified tropical diseases. We called the characteristic prison walk the "Cabanatuan shuffle": sick, emaciated, hopeless men shuffling slowly along, barely picking up their feet like old men in a total-care rest home. Malaria, dysentery, and beri-beri were everywhere. Men who could no longer control themselves or who were too sick to take care of themselves were laid under the barracks or out by the latrine to die. It was a common sight to see the swollen, discolored, decaying bodies of former soldiers and officers I had once known, lying in the grass, naked, waiting for the burial detail which already had more bodies than it could take care of. Men were no more than walking skeletons, and it even became painful to sit down on our thinly fleshed tail bones.

The so-called hospital was divided into wards: malaria, beri-beri, dysentery, and surgical. The dysentery ward was called the "Zero" ward, because to end up there was the finish, the end, "Zero." Almost everyone suffered from beri-beri, scurvy, or some vitamin deficiency. Many a man's hands were black, swollen, and cracked from pellagra; others could hardly eat because of sore mouths from scurvy. I saw many men with their legs swollen to twice their normal size from beri-beri. Everyone suffered from weak kidneys, and while many men were going to the latrine once every hour, it was common to make six trips a night. The latrines were filthy and crawling with maggots; there were no wells for bathing when we first arrived, and since it was the dry season, most men had not bathed in a long

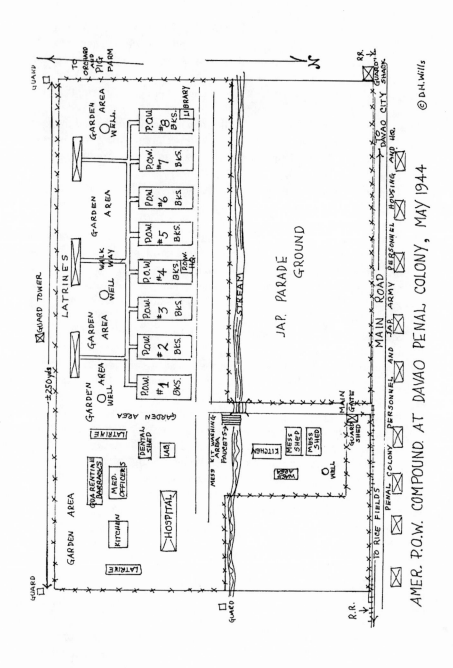

AMER. P.O.W. COMPOUND AT DAVAO PENAL COLONY, MAY 1944

© D.H.Wills

time. Later during the rainy season, we could at least take a bath under the eaves of the nipa shacks.

The men, desperate, ate anything. A dog or cat wandering into camp didn't last long. Frogs from the drainage ditches were eaten raw, contributing to dysentery. We even tried to make grass soup. To make grim matters worse, in August a diphtheria epidemic descended on the camp. Men choked to death. The death toll reached 50 on some days.

We dug mass graves, 30 men to a grave. As the rainy season came on, the land around and over the mass graves bubbled with gas. Now and then limbs would become visible as the gas propelled them up through the soggy earth. It was a nightmare and few except the grave details ventured near the cemetery.

The men could hardly do the fatigue details and interior guard duty that the Japanese insisted on. During these months there were reprisals for escapes and men were killed for various offenses. On two different work details at least, men were killed because other men escaped. On one work detail, Private Cowen of the Air Corps witnessed the shooting of ten men who died singing "God Bless America." Five Americans and two Filipinos were shot for bringing food into camp and selling it. They were killed after they had been tied out in the sun for several days and beaten. A Japanese firing squad executed them in full sight of the camp. A Jap officer delivered the coup de grâce.

A Colonel Biggs and three men were caught at the back fence, arguing about escape. These three were tied to poles in front of camp headquarters for several days. From time to time Jap guards came by to beat on them. One Jap officer untied the colonel and illustrated his competence at judo. This was in full view of the camp. I will never forget the sight of the burly Jap officer repeatedly slamming the old, emaciated, grey headed colonel to the ground. Each time the Jap would drag him to his feet again. I could hear the colonel beg, "Don't do this to me, I'm an old man." We were helpless to do anything, but my hate for the Japanese grew and I vowed that one day I would strike back and then I would show no mercy. Later the Japanese moved the three to the main road and tied them to stakes beside the guard house. Filipinos passing were required to beat on them. We could hear the men screaming throughout the night. Later they were taken off in a truck and we never saw or heard from them again.

The Japanese went out on patrol into the countryside often. We would hear shooting and we supposed that they were pursuing guerrillas. One day a patrol brought in two Filipino heads on sticks. These were hung at the

Opposite: **This sketch of American POW Camp #2 at Cabanatuan in central Luzon shows the layout of the camp when the POWs first arrived in May, 1942. The camp changed somewhat during the next three years.**

R.L

WAR DEPARTMENT

THE ADJUTANT GENERAL'S OFFICE

WASHINGTON

IN REPLY
REFER TO   AG 201 Wills, Donald H.
(12-12-42) PC-3   348114-3

December 30, 1942.

Mr. Charles H. Wills,
196 Huron Avenue,
Lynchburg, Virginia.

Dear Mr. Wills:

Report has been received that your son, First Lieutenant Donald Herbert Wills, O-389373, Cavalry, is now a prisoner of war of the Japanese Government in the Philippine Islands. This will confirm my telegram of December 15, 1942.

The Provost Marshal General, Prisoner of War Information Bureau, Washington, D.C., will furnish you the address to which mail may be sent. Any future correspondence in connection with his status as a prisoner of war should be addressed to that office.

Very truly yours,

A. ULIO
Major General,
The Adjutant General

1 Inclosure:
Memorandum re Financial Benefits.

This notice received by my parents gave welcome news that their son was alive, but began the long period of anxiety for his treatment and chances to survive.

headquarters building and left for several days, so we could all see how the Japanese treated resisters.

For the first time I began to doubt my chances for survival. We had given up hope for an American rescue, and I was resigned to settle in for a long hard fight to stay alive. The will to survive must be very strong. Most of the prisoners, in spite of the depressing and inhumane conditions to which we were subjected, kept busy trying to keep living. In spite of knowing that even a minor illness would likely mean death, we didn't have time to think about it. We were too busy. We became hardened to death and took the daily grave details as a matter of course in a detached way. It's almost impossible to describe, but my feeling was: "It's happening to those other poor guys but not to me!" Looking back after nearly fifty years, it is hard for me to believe it all happened, but I know that it did.

My hepatitis condition had improved. A fellow prisoner, a doctor, told me to eat as much sugar as I could get hold of and to take a laxative every day. I had magnesium sulfate in my store of medicines and I took a dose every day and ate what coconut candy I could buy or trade from other prisoners. The Japanese had begun to sell some in camp. Although still jaundiced, I was able to move around and contact friends.

I found Captain Richards, a former roommate. He had been an animation artist for Disney Studios before the war and my roommate at Ft. Stotsenburg. Captain LeBrun of the 60th Coast Artillery shared my barracks as did Captain Mills of the Philippine Scouts infantry. Captain Cecil LeBrun, of French Canadian descent and totally bilingual, lived on the border between Maine and Canada. He had been with the Coast Artillery on Corregidor. Capt. Buster Mills, a Californian, had been with the Philippine Scouts infantry.

Because I had some medicines, I held sick call in the barracks for the other 99 men. I shared the medicines in my corpsman's bag and picked up the nickname "Doc." I treated bacillary dysentery with sulfathiozol, infections with iodine, merthiolate, sulfanilamide, and Mercurochrome. Vitamins were the most valuable item we had, but the store we had scrounged from on Bataan was not nearly enough. Finally, I had to stop sick call since supplies were running low. I wanted to save some for myself and a few close friends. I also discovered that the medicines we had shared when we had to divide them at San Fernando were being sold to prisoners at five pesos a pill!

We battled constantly to get enough to eat and almost every waking hour we spent figuring out how to use almost anything for food. We quickly learned that we could eat carabao blood. When the Japs had us butcher a carabao for them, we would catch the blood in canteen cups when the throat was cut. We would set the cup by the fire and let the blood congeal. Then we dumped out the lump of blood, sliced it, and put it on our rice or fried it and ate it with our rice.

After mess call one day, I passed an Air Corps lieutenant who had something in a canteen cup. He was sitting in the shade of the barracks with his serving of rice and soup. Emaciated and only skin and bones, he held his cup up for me to see. It was full of brownish red-earthworms which he had already heated up over a fire.

"Try one," he said, "They're full of protein."

I took one and put it on my rice. It was like eating a stick of mud. We later learned to wash the worms and squeeze the mud out of them before cooking them. Another time a fellow prisoner showed me his canteen cup containing two big, whitish carabao eyes. I asked him what he was going to do with them.

"I'm going to eat them," he said. "They're full of vitamins."

We were even reduced to trying to eat grass. We boiled up the blades in a canteen cup, but we couldn't digest the grass and the green water wasn't even as good as kangkong soup.

A friend, Lieutenant Ward from the cavalry, who lived in another part of the camp, came down with cerebral malaria. He had previously borrowed five pesos from me to buy coconut candy. One day I went to his barracks to see him. He was lying in one corner of the barracks on the floor and I could tell he was desperately ill. He could hardly sit up. We talked for a while, but there was not much I could do. He paid me the five pesos. A couple of days later, I went back to see him. He was gone. One of the men told me he had died the day before. I felt guilty because I had taken the five pesos.

The days dragged on. The death toll had dropped to around fifteen a day. The rainy season had come and made everything gloomier, if possible. A typhoon crossed central Luzon and blew into camp. The high winds threatened to blow off our roof. Several of us climbed on top of the barracks to hold down the nipa roofing. The temperature dropped rapidly and the high wind and driving rain seemed terribly cold. I caught a bad chest cold and it hung on for weeks. I still believe it developed into pleurisy, as I had bad congestion and chest pains for weeks. Of course we had no warm clothes, only ragged shirts, pants or shorts, and slippers or old shoes.

In late August all Americans of the rank of full colonel and above were moved out of camp bound for Japan. The Japanese began to give the hospital a little more medicine, some from Java and even old stuff from Bataan. Boredom set in. Available singers, musicians, and actors formed groups to entertain the other prisoners. Members of the Sigma Alpha Epsilon college fraternity put together a program to relieve the gloom and boredom. In spite of the grim and depressing conditions, the shows were well attended. It was good to hear the audience applaud. The shows were given from a bamboo platform built behind the barracks and were put on at regular intervals.

About this time we were given printed POW cards so that we could send a message home. We could not describe the conditions, but could only send our love and say that we were well. The cards had blanks that were to be filled in. I wrote that I was well and reported my weight at 135 pounds. Since my normal weight was 185, I knew my parents would understand my situation. Everyone tried to work some secret message into the few words that could be written on the cards.

About this time Cecil (Captain LeBrun) and I decided to try out a couple of work details. Actually, the only one we went out on was the wood-gathering detail. Our Jap guard on several trips was a Lieutenant Okubo. He spoke English and had been a bank teller in Osaka before the war. During our rest breaks he was anxious to talk. He even gave me his home address in Osaka. He always brought along a canteen of hot tea which he shared with us. It was weak green tea but it sure tasted good.

In October the Japanese selected 1,000 men to go to Japan. They wanted technicians, machinists, welders, and other skilled labor. Thank goodness, I did not fit their specifications.

Shortly thereafter, another rumor floated around camp that the Japanese also wanted 1,000 men to go south to Mindanao to work at the Davao Penal Colony. The idea of going south sounded good to me – 700 miles farther south, closer to Australia and American forces. I talked to the American sergeant who was making up the list for the camp commander and told him to put me on the list. Only healthy prisoners were being taken. I was over my malaria and hepatitis and in pretty good shape, so I got on the roster.

October 26, 1942, our gear was loaded on trucks and we 1,000 volunteers marched into Cabanatuan. Once again we boarded freight cars for the trip to Manila. From the station we marched to Bilibid prison once again. After another night on the cement floors, we marched to the harbor where we boarded a rusty old 5,000-ton former American tramp steamer. We later found a plate on the side of the superstructure which listed "Erie" as the place of the ship's origin. We referred to it as the "Erie Maru." Probably it was one that had been sold to the Japanese before the war, along with all the scrap iron that they had bought and were now shooting back at us. The old steamer they converted to a troop ship. We were assigned to the aft welldeck and hold. The Japanese were loading Filipinos, men and women, into the forward welldeck. We suffered in the steamy heat until October 28, when we moved out into the bay. It took us several hours to cross Manila Bay. We passed Corregidor close enough to see the devastation from the bombardment of those 600 guns around the hospital on Bataan and from the aerial bombing.

Along each side of our hold the Japs had built a wooden platform that ran the length and doubled the capacity. On the main deck space above the

IMPERIAL JAPANESE ARMY

1. I am interned at—Philippine Military Prison Camp No. ____2____

2. My health is—excellent; good; fair; poor.

3. Message (50 words limit)

Hope you are all well. Waiting to hear from you.

Write c/o International Red Cross. So far I'm OK.

_____ _____ Tell all my friends I'm well

& all love to you, Dad, Len, Charles. See you soon.

Love. _____   *Donald H. Wilbs*
                             Signature

This POW card, courtesy of the Japanese Imperial Army, enabled us to send home some scant information about our situation and health at Cabanatuan POW Camp #2 in August of 1942. Unfortunately the card was not delivered until some time in late 1944.

hold, we could sleep topside where it was cooler. In the daytime we sat around on the cargo booms. The Japanese were being lenient for a change and we could move around on the welldeck. On rainy nights we slept in the hold and some of us moved into the midship hold and slept on piles of coal. There was one drawback to sleeping below deck, especially in the coal bunker. The ship was swarming with cockroaches, the big flying kind one or two inches long. They came out at night and crawled all over us while we slept. After brushing them off my face a few times, I learned to sleep with a piece of cloth covering my head. Even then I could feel them running over me all night. I also learned that they can bite, a kind of "nip" once in a while.

The Japs recruited prisoners to clean not only our areas but the Japanese areas of the ship as well. We were allowed to move around freely except to the area where the Filipinos were held.

There was plenty of rice on board and our ration improved. Many of the prisoners still suffered from diarrhea but seemed to improve as the days passed. We were getting four or five bags of rice for each of our two meals a day. The food detail dumped the rice into a drum and washed it three times. Then it was put into a big kawa (pot) where it was cooked over a wood fire on deck. There was an ice locker aboard containing fish and carabao meat. The catch was—no ice! The meat went bad quickly in the tropical heat. It turned green and finally had to be thrown out, but not before we had eaten quite a lot of it and got diarrhea all over again. The Japs gave us corned beef from the drums of corned beef (U.S. naval stores) on board. Again, it was half spoiled but we ate it anyway. We also had pickled Japanese cabbage and once in a while the Japs would give us a cask of pickled plums which were very salty, but we counted ourselves lucky to get them.

Our toilet was a three-holer built over the ship rail. The location of these latrines was later to come in handy.

Captain LeBrun and I, on the food detail, washed about five bags of rice for each meal. The Japs scheduled the meals and ruled that the officers were to be fed first, enlisted men afterward. This caused somewhat of a confrontation. The enlisted men assembled on deck and sang during "officers' mess": "I don't want to go to the circus, I want to watch the officers eat." The enlisted men got the same ration, but resented the fact that the officers were being served first. It was a friendly rivalry as we were all prisoners together, a fact that none of us could forget.

I saw Lieutenant Okubo, the former bank teller from Osaka. He informed me that he was making the trip as translator and would be with us at Davao.

The ship made its way into the South China Sea, south past Mindoro Island, and passed through the Sibuyan Sea, and stopped at Iloilo on Panay where some of the Filipinos disembarked. We sailed around Negros and pulled into Cebu where the rest of the Filipinos went ashore. We traveled on by Bohol Island and through the Surigao Straits. We then moved down the east coast of Mindanao which is roadless and seldom visited as it is populated by a few barrios of different Philippine tribes. In this area we sailed over the famous Mindanao Deep, the deepest part of the Pacific Ocean.

On November 7, 1942, we rounded Cape San Agustin and headed up in Davao Gulf. We landed at Davao City where we disembarked onto the dock. After a short wait and a head count, we loaded into open-back trucks and stood up for the 30-mile trip to Davao Penal Colony at the upper end of the Davao Gulf. The 13 days on board the "Erie Maru" had been a great improvement over Cabanatuan. It had almost been a pleasant boat trip. We now were looking forward with hope for a better life at Davao Penal Colony. Anything would be an improvement over Cabanatuan.

4. Davao Prison Camp

WHEN we arrived at the Davao Penal Colony, a few of the administrative personnel were still there. The Filipino convicts originally housed at the Davao Colony had been moved elsewhere by the Japanese. The few still around were mostly servants for the remaining officials. On the three square miles the Colony covered, the convicts had raised all of their own food. In this relatively uninhabited part of the island of Mindanao, areas had been cleared to raise farm products: an extensive rice-growing area, a banana plantation, an abaca plantation, areas planted to guava, avocado, papaya, and other tropical fruits. There were ponds for raising fish, a rice mill, a pig farm, chicken farms, a sawmill, and a number of cattle.

Symbolically the road into camp terminated at the penal headquarters. It was certainly a dead-end for us prisoners who ended up there. Deep jungle surrounded the extensive clearing for the Colony. The clustered nipa and weathered wooden buildings against the background of the green jungle gave the promise of possible escape. On the north side of the road were the administrative building and the building for the employees. On the other side of the road were the barracks for the prisoners, much like the ones at Cabanatuan. These, however, were much better built with corrugated roofs. There were eight barracks which housed about 200 men each, 12 in each of the 16 bays which comprised the layout of the barracks.

A large mess shed with tables and benches and a cooking area behind it was located beyond the barracks, a far cry from the primitive open fires and serving kawas at Cabanatuan. The hospital buildings were across a small creek at the south end of the row of barracks. There was a main building and several smaller ones, all built of bamboo, sawali, and nipa palm leaves.

The three camp latrines were at the rear to the south of the row of barracks, far enough back so that there was a small garden area between the barracks and the latrines. Here also were three open wells and wooden platforms for bathing. The latrines were well-built sheds of about 10 holes each, luxurious when compared to the maggot-infested, fly-covered slit trenches at our old camp. There were water taps at the small creek as well as a wooden trough where we could wash our mess kits. We no longer had to wait in line only to find the water turned off.

The barracks had wide overhanging corrugated roofs on each side and during the frequent rains we stood under these to take our showers. Prisoners had a living area in the bays on each side of the center walkway and bunks were double and, in some cases, triple deck. In front of the barracks was a gravel walkway. Camp headquarters was installed in the middle building, and the camp was surrounded by a barbed wire fence.

The entrance gate to the camp was in front of the mess hall. In addition to some dirt roads throughout the colony, there was a narrow gauge railroad which ran the length of the penal colony from the rice fields on one side to the farm and logging area on the other side, a distance of eight or ten kilometers.

The camp was clean and neat; the latrines newly built (by the convicts before they left) and, except for the infestation of bedbugs (which we soon discovered), the camp was a tremendous improvement over Cabanatuan. With all the food around, we looked forward to relatively luxurious living! What a comedown we were to have!

The Japanese commander, Major Maeda, had come in from Malaybalay in Mindanao, along with the 1,000 other prisoners who had arrived two weeks before us. These consisted of Americans who had been serving with the Philippine Army in Mindanao and who had been captured in Mindanao at the surrender and concentrated at Malaybalay, a town in Cagayan province in central Mindanao. Our camp was highly organized. The ranking American officer was in command of the American prisoners, taking his orders from the Japanese commander who supervised the whole operation including the Filipino prison employees.

The Jap commander gave personnel requirements for work details to the American commander who worked out the assignments on the different details. For the most part the American commander posted job options and took volunteers. The options were railroad detail, sawmill gang, jungle bajuco detail, pig farm, chicken farm, machine shop, rice mill, farm detail, rice field detail, banana plantation, and a number of other smaller details that were made up from time to time.

The food ration at first was reasonably adequate, especially when compared to Cabanatuan. As the months went on, however, we were back down to rice and kangkong soup. However, we did have more frequent issues of beef or fish. Most food that was grown in the colony went to the Japanese troops in the colony and in Davao. Consequently we became rather adept at "quaning" food: chickens, fruit, whatever became reachable. *Quan* is Tagalog for "appropriating," or without euphemism, "stealing."

I saw Lieutenant Okubo from time to time. He would always ask, "How awe you?, Lieutenant Weeus." He was a pleasant Japanese, I must admit, and I intended to use him if I could as he seemed to take a liking to me. He even asked me to make a sketch of him, which I did.

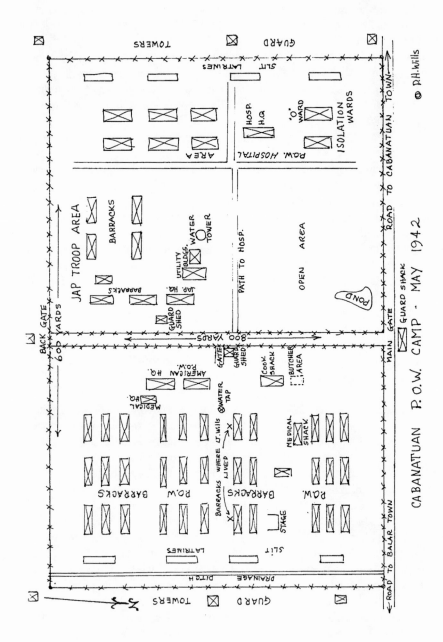

CABANATUAN P.O.W. CAMP - MAY 1942   © P.H.Wills

In November, 1942, a neighboring abaca plantation asked for 100 volunteers, and Cecil LeBrun, Lieutenant Young, and I signed up for the Furakawa Plantation detail. This civilian enterprise was about 40 miles south of Davao. We traveled by the usual Japanese open-bed truck.

Here facilities were even nicer than ours at the penal colony. The building was new, recently built, clean, and large enough for 100 prisoners. We had enough to eat and the Japanese and Filipino civilians were not too unpleasant, although they avoided contact with us. The Japanese had told us that we would work in the shade inside the big factory where fibers were macerated and soaked before being made into rope. Of course we worked outside in the abaca fields.

The abaca plants are banana-like trees, some with trunks a foot in diameter. We cut these down and loaded the trunks on trucks. The work day began at 6 a.m., lasted until noon, then resumed at 2 and lasted until 6. We worked seven days a week so that we could have three free days at Christmas.

We cut down the abaca plants with large bolos (machetes) which were issued to us each morning and collected at night. Abaca harvesting was rough, backbreaking work. The heavy trunks had to be trimmed off at the top and then carried out to the road and loaded on the trucks, sometimes a distance of 100 yards or more with trunks weighing up to 150 pounds. The trees were full of spiders, ants, and centipedes. One of the centipedes bit a large, blustery Chicagoan, Sergeant Tonelli, on the upper arm. His arm swelled painfully, and he was unable to work for several days. The centipede measured about eight inches in length!

While working at the Furakawa Plantation, we felt more like slaves than prisoners of war. Our guards were civilians and few soldiers were in evidence. Only a small detachment lived at the plantation. The Japanese civilians were more pleasant to work for than the soldiers, but nonetheless, we were required to work long hard hours. We were herded along in groups and there was no doubt as to who was the dominant race.

The detail ended when we had harvested all the mature abaca. After two months we returned to Davao, on January 12, 1943. We were assigned to new barracks and put on the rice detail, the worst of all details. Nevertheless, every able-bodied prisoner up to the age of 45 spent some time on this backbreaking work. We planted, weeded, and harvested 600 acres. The work crews formed up before daylight and got on the narrow gauge train which took us to the rice fields, about 10 kilometers away. We worked until noon, had two hours off, then worked until dusk.

Rice fields are a lousy place to work. The fields vary in size from one to

Opposite: **This sketch shows the layout of the American POW camp at Davao Penal Colony on Mindanao Island, in 1942–1944.**

three or four acres and are surrounded by mud dikes. The dry fields are flooded and become mud. We worked up to the waist in this mud, barefooted, and wearing only a "fandochi" or G-string. We gathered seedlings from the seed patches, selected one plant from our bunch, and stuck it in the mud. This was repeated over and over until the field was planted in rows. This messy, malodorous job continued constantly because the fields were planted, weeded, and harvested in rotation. After harvest we plowed with carabao (water buffalo) which pulled a platform with vertical wooden stakes. These stirred up the mud and dead vegetation and pushed the weeds under, then the field was ready to plant again. After planting the seedlings, the fields had to be weeded by hand until the rice achieved a good height. Then it crowded out the weeds. At harvest, using a carved knife, we cut off the stems of grain and put them in large baskets. These we loaded on the train and sent them to the rice mill. Since the rice field work requires the laborer to lean over all the time, we all had aching backs. Our legs were continually cut or scratched and everyone had rice hash – red bumps along the scratches from the ankles to the crotch. I have simplified here the description of rice-detail work; it was much more detailed and nasty.

Intestinal parasites became a way of life. Hookworm, which makes a red mark where it enters, was the most common offender. Prisoners working on the farm and on the pig detail also picked up hookworms. Actually intestinal parasites were one of the most common ailments in camp. This ailment was largely ignored as it was seldom life threatening.

During our two-hour lunch break, we lay around on the dikes and ate our lunches of rice brought out from camp. Mickey, an Irishman from the 31st Infantry, gave us a good laugh on one occasion. He was an ex-boxer with thick brows, a squashed nose, and cauliflower ears.

Quite a few of the Japanese soldiers liked to show off. There was one in particular, we called him "Speedo," who thought he was a "tough egg." He was always giving us trouble. His favorite trick was to show us in a few minutes how fast he could do our work, then he would spend the rest of the day yelling at us to work faster. Hence the name "Speedo."

We had our tough guys also, men who would do anything on a bet, and one day Speedo made the mistake of picking on one of them, Mickey. It happened during the planting season. Anywhere from 400 to 500 Americans were out every day working in the paddies. One morning during our 10-minute rest period, Speedo, who could speak a little English, decided he would show us how tough he was.

We were sitting around on the dikes resting. His claim that day was that he could let any one of us hit him in the stomach as hard as we were able and it wouldn't hurt him. Warming up to the subject, he dared any of us to hit him. We didn't like the idea, afraid that we would get into trouble, although there wasn't one of us who didn't want to take the opportunity.

Mickey, the former boxer and ready for anything, acted more interested than the rest of us, so Speedo urged him to try. Mickey hesitated, but when the Jap said he would give him a peso to do it, that was too much. With deadly aim, and putting all the strength of his skinny body into the blow, Mickey buried his fist in the Jap's solar-plexus. Like a deflating balloon, Speedo collapsed on the dike and his rifle splashed into the paddy. Mickey quickly recovered the rifle, laid it on the dike beside Speedo, and commenced splashing water in his face. A Japanese sergeant, seeing the commotion, came running over and demanded to know what happened. When he heard the story, he was really mad. Speedo had recovered by this time and the sergeant ordered him to his feet.

Recovering his muddy rifle, Speedo came to attention. The sergeant, in the usual disciplinary manner of the Japanese army, proceeded to give him hell for becoming too familiar with American prisoners, punctuating his remarks with slaps from his open hand. Then he ordered Speedo back to his barracks. Speedo marched off, having completely lost face in front of several hundred grinning Americans, and for the next few days at least, he was a very meek Jap. Mickey was the only man I knew of who got away with kayoing a Japanese guard!

When I was finally relieved of work in the paddies, I was assigned to the rice mill. The rice from the paddies was laid out on mats to dry for several days. Then it had to be threshed and put through the dehusking machine. It was then put into 100-kilo sacks and stored in warehouses. The prisoners ran the machines under the direction of the Japanese, and we prisoners also loaded and stored the sacks in a bodega (warehouse).

I came down with malaria again. It was the vivax type giving chills, fever, headaches, and heavy sweating. After about eight hours, the fever would subside. Then another attack would follow. This lasted from ten to thirty days and then subsided and became dormant until another attack months later.

I was sent to the north barracks about half a mile away where the Japs now tried to isolate malaria patients. These barracks were behind a square, triple-wire fence and had formerly been for dangerous criminals. The barracks buildings formed a star in the middle of the compound. The Japanese were now using this section to isolate medical patients or as a punishment area.

Here we slept in bunks, the same as those used by the former Filipino prisoners. These were wooden, in three tiers, and were screened against mosquitoes. We reached the top bunks by ladder and all bunks had sliding doors. The screens kept out the mosquitoes, but the bunks were full of bedbugs which hid in the cracks in the daytime but came out at night. Their bite left a red itchy spot and those with bad cases had bites all over their bodies. We hated them and spent lots of time trying to dig them out of the cracks.

When they were crushed, they gave off an unpleasant, musky smell. To this day the mention of a bedbug brings back loathesome memories.

I was taking five to six hundred milligrams of quinine a day, so I stayed in bed most of the time, weak with no appetite, dizzy, and with a constant ringing in the head because of large doses of quinine. Finally, after fifteen or twenty days, the malaria began to subside and became dormant. I returned to the main camp, somewhat thinner but feeling good. I was assigned to new barracks.

Meals had deteriorated into the old rice and kangkong soup routine. Since this was a cattle farm, there were hundreds of carabao and brahma steers, but we got almost no beef. The Japs butchered frequently for themselves, and we were still getting the old "NRA" issue. When cooked up for 2,000 men, this didn't go very far, just a dipper full of grey stew on your pile of watery rice.

I signed up for the banana detail which provided an opportunity to quan some fruit. We cut down the ripe bunches of bananas and hauled them out to the road to be picked up by a bull cart. Of course we missed no opportunity to eat lots of ripe bananas on the way to the road. The trunks were cut down and the roots dug up and divided into four parts. We then replanted the divided roots for the new crop.

Across from the prison lived a prison employee who had remained. We went to this house to get water from their tap to fill our canteens. The Filipina housewife made fried bananas which she gave to us almost every day. She rolled the bananas in rice paste and deep fried them in coconut oil and wrapped them in banana leaves. She would pass us a few when we came to get water. She was kind but distant and careful. She obviously did not want to be seen being kind to us by the Japanese.

On the back porch she had big jars filled with banana skins, water, and sour rice paste which she let ferment to produce a vinegar. It didn't take us long to adopt her method back in camp to make our own vinegar. Using the vinegar, we could add chili peppers for our own "Tabasco." It sure made that plain rice taste better. Soon all the barracks had bottles of it cooking on the shelves in the sun.

On the banana detail we usually ate our lunch under a nipa shed beside the road and across the road from the fried-banana lady's house on the edge of the banana plantation. One time when we had gathered for lunch, we saw Sergeant Tonelli coming down the path with a chicken in his hand. We had a fire going to warm up our rice, and we now anticipated some roast chicken. When he was about ten feet from the fire, a Jap guard suddenly came out of a side trail; Sergeant Tonelli stopped cold while holding the chicken by the neck. The guard stopped, stared, and yelled: "Nanika?" (what are you doing?). Tonelli hesitated a second, opened his hand to let the chicken drop, and said defensively, "I don't know nothin' about it."

The chicken ran off under the banana trees. The Jap guard stood open-mouthed for a moment, then shrugged and walked off. We ate our rice without chicken that day. However, it was a good detail while it lasted for a couple of weeks.

In February, 1943, I decided to try the pig-feeding detail. I had begun to think daily about escaping. The pig farm was a short distance away (about a kilometer) and a Jap guard picked us up each morning. We first filled up some large baskets with kangkong, then we proceeded through a guava orchard where we could gather plenty of ripe guavas as we went through. The pigs were in pens scattered around in an avocado orchard. A few chicken houses stood here and there, and the eggs had to be gathered each day. Needless to say, we became adept at quickly puncturing, sucking the eggs, and burying the crushed shells in the foot-deep mud. The avocado trees offered big purple avocados which were another bonus. While the guard was at the other end of the pig farm, we could shinny up a tree to gather a few avocados to stash away and eat at our leisure. This time the pigs ate the kangkong.

I next rotated to the farm detail which turned out to be one of the least desired details. We weeded squash fields or cassava fields, and at harvest time we loaded trucks with squash or cassava roots. We couldn't find much to quan at the produce farm, and the harvest went to Davao and the Japanese and very little of it to our kitchen. There was no chance of escaping. We were too closely watched.

Back at camp the evening issue of rice depended on where we worked. Rice field workers received the biggest issue, other detail workers got a medium portion, and men who stayed in camp for one reason or another (sick or administrative) received the smallest portion. On his birthday a prisoner got a large issue of rice. Working on a detail where we could quan extra food was much preferred over the rice field, farm, lumber, or bajuco details.

Once, the Japanese put out the word that they wanted some men who were divers. I had been an intramural swimmer and a life guard at Virginia Beach during college, so I volunteered along with four or five other prisoners. With two Jap guards, we would ride the railroad past the rice fields and on out to the terminal at the west fork of the Salug River which emptied into the upper end of Davao Gulf. At first, this sounded like it had escape possibilities.

We were to dive for freshwater clams. A launch waited for us with two empty 55-gallon drums on board. We had no goggles, fins, or anything else except our hands. The water was only ten or fifteen feet deep, luke warm, and dark brown or black from decaying vegetation. It was a typical slow-flowing stream with thick jungle and swamp on each side. The launch moved up and down the stream until we found a bed of clams. We then had to dive down with a basket and dig around in the slime of the bottom for the clams which congregated in colonies.

We came up for air and dumped our clams into the drums. We had to fill the two 55-gallon drums before we could go back to camp. The Japs allowed us to eat clams for lunch and we could also put a few clams in our sack. This detail didn't last long. We went out only six or eight times. The clams went to the Japanese officers' mess. It was surprising how quickly five or six of us could fill the two drums. We were usually on the way back to camp at 3 or 4 in the afternoon. This detail turned out to be OK for food but impossible for escape, too many guards, too much swamp. We could not have gotten out of the boat and through the swamp without a shot in the back. I always figured that those clams were the most nutritious food that we were able to obtain. The clams or mussels were of good size, about as big as the cherrystone variety of salt water clams in America.

In February, 1943, the Japanese announced that they would pay us for working. We were to receive 200 pesos per month. We were to be paid 10 or 15 percent in cash and the rest was to be placed in a Philippine bank in our name so that we could receive the funds after the war. There was, of course, a considerable deduction for room and board! Considering the accommodations and the cuisine, this was a joke!

In March of 1943, we received our first Red Cross packages from Davao. Most of the packages came from the South African, Australian, or New Zealand Red Cross with a few from the American Red Cross. Each man got about one-half of each kind. We each ended up with about three tropical chocolate bars, a can of cheese (3 to 4 oz.), a can of dried milk, some prunes, two or three cans of corned beef, a can of Spam, soluble coffee, a box of sugar cubes, bouillon powder, a small can of sardines, a can of jam, a 4 oz. can of butter, a can of mutton, and a can of corned pork. I used the three or four packages of cigarettes to trade for more chocolate. I immediately made up an escape packet of three bars of chocolate, a can of corned beef, and a can of sardines. The rest was put to good use over the following months to upgrade our rice and kangkong diet.

About this time our captors also set up in camp little stores which stocked leaf tobacco, brown sugar candy, fried bananas, and other Filipino goodies. In these "shops" we could spend our newly acquired funds. Red Cross cards were also passed out so that we could send messages home. On these cards were the usual blanks you could fill in to tell about prison camp. Delivery, however, was very slow. When I arrived home in late 1945, my card from Davao arrived soon after!

I had become friendly with a Filipino convict who had remained at the camp and with whom I was able to talk from time to time in the past year. He was in for murder. One day, casually, he asked if I would be interested in escaping. It took me by surprise, and I told him I had to think about it.

I wasn't sure how to take the offer and whether or not it might be a trap. I told him I would let him know.

My best friend, Cecil LeBrun, was sick. I knew he couldn't make the escape and I didn't want to take off without him, as in those days friendships were very close. The Filipino told me not to wait too long. Shortly thereafter, in March on a Sunday, 12 men with two Filipinos, one of whom was my friend, escaped. These men, led by Commander McCoy of the Navy and Lieutenant Greshio of the Air Corps, had been working on the coffee detail close to camp. They went out every day and the inmate, a trusty, accompanied them rather than a Jap guard. The group was not missed until that evening. As soon as the Japanese learned of the escape, they suspended all work details and locked us in camp. Truckloads of soldiers searched the colony for four or five days but could not find the escapees.

As punishment, the men in the escapees' barracks were moved to the malaria north compound. Rations to everyone were cut in half and only a few essential work details resumed, going out under heavy guard. However, in a couple of weeks things returned to normal. But not for me; I kept on kicking myself for not accepting the Filipino's offer and going with the escapees.

After the escape a new work detail became available: fence building. The Japanese were constructing a new barbed wire fence around additional parts of the colony. I volunteered for this detail. Anything for a change. We cut kapok trees for fence posts. These trees are 40 to 50 feet tall with trunks up to a foot or more in diameter and covered with stubby thorns. Pods of kapok grew on the branches. Kapok is used in life preservers, so we would also harvest the ripe pods to be sent to Davao for processing.

We cut the trees down with an axe and had to carry the trunks to where the fence was being built. The posts were green and about ten feet long and were very heavy. When sunk, only six or eight feet were above ground. Before we cut down the tree, we had to climb up and top it out, all the while trying to avoid the sharp spines. After planting, the posts were so green and the ground so damp that they began to grow. Within a few weeks the new branches had to be cut back. This detail, of course, gave no chance of escape. The Japanese were more alert and watchful, and we were working close in with many guards around.

The weeks kept dragging and we tried many work details to break the monotony. After we completed the fence, I volunteered for the bajuco detail. Bajuco (rattan) is a vine that can be finger-size to two inches in diameter. This vine is covered with a sheath of leaves that have vicious spines.

We went by rail to the jungle area, roamed out into the jungle until we found a patch of vines, and then worked half a day or until each man had fulfilled his quota of about 20 twenty-foot-long sections. We had to cut our way into the jungle with bolos to find the patches and then decide if the vines were big enough (one inch in diameter or more). We used the bolo to cut the vine off at the ground. We cut off enough of the sheath so that we could grab the vine and then pull it down out of the trees which could be as tall as 50 feet or 100 feet. We had to back away as we pulled the vine down and then take care not to step on the spines that we had stripped off the sheathing. On our feet we were wearing only wooden clogs. We then cut the vines in 20-foot lengths.

We also had to watch out for snakes and insects since spiders and centipedes were everywhere. We were usually showered with these as we pulled the vines down.

Our food rations were continuing to deteriorate to 1,000 to 1,200 calories a day, mostly starch. We should have been getting more than 2,000 calories for the kind of work we were doing, as well as much more protein. The average man was 30 to 50 pounds lighter than his usual weight.

We could get no word from the outside world. The Japanese told us that they were winning, but we guessed that things were not going too well for them. One week they would tell us that they had defeated us at Bougainville and a few weeks later, they would say they had defeated us at Lae, New Guinea. We knew that MacArthur was moving up the island chain.

One of my friends was a Dr. Peters who worked in the hospital area. He was a dentist and, with his antiquated equipment, he took care of the camp dental needs. His drill was a World War I field type, worked by a foot pedal. His supply of zinc oxide and oil of cloves and amalgam had recently been augmented by a shipment of medicines issued to the hospital by the Japanese. Some of these supplies were stored in boxes in Dr. Peters' shack. Dr. Peters had filled a couple of teeth for me, and during my visits to his office, we talked guardedly about escaping. I was feeling him out as I knew that some day I was going to have to make my escape attempt. I thought he would be a good one to have along because of his access to medicines which could be critical in any escape attempt, as an extended stay in the jungle was a distinct possibility before friendly natives could be contacted.

We both agreed that it was a military man's duty to escape if possible. He confided, however, that he was probably too old. He was a major and possibly in his early forties, while I was just 25.

To me it seemed strange, but at that time not many of the prisoners were planning escape. The general psychology seemed to be: "If I can just stay alive and wait this out, I might be liberated and returned home." Few seemed to realize that up to that time, fewer than 25 percent of the POWs in all wars survived to be liberated or returned home!

In the boxes in Major Peters' shack were stored atabrine, emetine, Nembutal, some sulfa drugs, and other medicines and medical equipment.

At this time we had a good supply of medicines for the camp and sickness was actually fairly low except for the continuing chronic malaria, dysentery, intestinal parasites, and other relatively minor sickness. Dysentery was not dangerous if sulfa and emetine were available.

Because he knew that I was really planning an escape, Major Peters, on one of my visits, when he had finished filling a small molar cavity with amalgam (which, incidentally, lasted many years), said he had to run an errand and left me in the office. He knew I wanted some of those medicines, and I rationalized the taking of them because I was going to use them in an escape to rejoin forces fighting against the Japanese. At a later date the medicines came in handy. When Major Peters returned a few minutes later, I had already quaned the medical supplies.

Back on the farm detail, we had a windfall. During lunch breaks, we came into a shed where the two old tractors were parked. The Japanese went off a way to have their lunch, and we ate our rice ration in this shed. The tractors were being run on grain alcohol made from sugar cane. We quickly decided that this alcohol was drinkable. A couple of prisoners watched out for the guards while I worked on the tractors. The fuel pump had a bowl underneath. I could loosen the retaining screw and the alcohol would run out of the tank through the fuel pump. We filled our canteens with the grain alcohol and took it back into camp. It had a strong gasoline taste because, of course, the tractors had originally been run on gasoline.

Since it took about 125 proof to run the engine, we cut the alcohol to half with water. We stayed on this detail for a couple of weeks and became bootleggers, trading our wares for other stuff in camp. We celebrated Christmas, 1943, with alcohol from the tractors.

Since I was an amateur herpetologist, I was always looking for snakes. One time, by the shower area, I caught a black and yellow Philippine cobra about two-and-a-half feet long. I took the snake back behind the barracks in the garden plot area and milked the cobra's venom into a little bottle. I got about one-half cc. I figured there must be some way I could use this poison on the guards, but I had to find out how lethal it was.

I had a small hypodermic syringe, and I caught a cat which was roaming around camp. I took it out to the garden area between the barracks and the latrines where we had an eggplant garden. I took one-fourth cc of venom in the syringe, cut it to one cc with alcohol, and injected one-fourth cc into the cat's back. In about 15 minutes the cat was wobbly and then it keeled over and died. Cobra venom is potent and works on the nervous system, paralyzing its victim. I never figured out a way to use the poison against our captors, however. I disposed of the dead cat in spite of an urge to cook it up!

In the fall of 1943, malaria had become prevalent again, and we were lucky that we had the additional Red Cross supplies and old U.S. Army supplies that the Japanese had issued to the camp. Our medical personnel had convinced the Japs to increase our rations for the sick. They provided some eggs, carabao milk, extra rice, and made some additional medicine available. At this time, deaths in camp had almost been eliminated. The weak had already died and we now had a stronger group who could survive.

The American headquarters commander tried to find books for the prisoners to read and to establish a library. The commander requested that everyone turn in books to be deposited in the library facility. The Japanese were asked and they had some books brought in from the former prison officials' libraries. Some Japanese and English magazines were also furnished. The newspapers that we saw were many months old, but we could tell that the war was not going well for the Japanese. As we had suspected, battle lines were moving toward the Philippines.

In October of 1943, the Japanese announced that the Philippines were to be a part of the Greater East Asia Co-Prosperity Sphere. Under this plan the Philippines would be granted independence. In December of 1943, this event was celebrated. We had a day off from work and our rations for the day were increased. We got an extra portion of rice, and the Japanese allowed us to butcher a carabao for our meal. In addition, some more old magazines were issued to the library.

In late 1943 two prisoners disappeared from a work detail in a heavy rainstorm. The Japanese later announced that they had been killed by natives. After my escape, I found out that they had survived.

About this time, early 1944, Maj. Charlie Harrison confided to me that he was planning to escape. He approached me in the garden area back of the barracks. This place was more private and out of sight and hearing of the guards or other prisoners.

"Herb, there's only one guard on the main gate when we go to eat. It seems to me this would be a good time and place to escape."

"Look, Charlie, that would be in full view of everyone in the mess hall and there are Jap guards not more than 150 yards down the road at the guard shack. The jungle is a few hundred yards back of the row of houses across the road, but you'll have a 250-yard run from the camp gate. Remember, the guards have rifles."

"I'll grab the Jap's rifle, run across the road and through the line of houses and into the jungle," his face radiated hope.

This plan sounded too desperate to me. How could he be sure he would subdue the guard and grab his rifle in just a few seconds before the alarm would be sounded? Even once in the jungle that close to camp, the Japanese could surround the area and cut him off.

"Charlie, I really don't like the plan. You'd better think it over some

EXTRA: Davao Times

INDEPENDENCE PROMISED TO P. I. THIS YEAR

TOKYO, June 16 (Domei)—Premier Hideki Tozyo, speaking before the House of Peers on the opening day of the 3-day 82nd extraordinary session of the Diet from 2 o'clock this afternoon, declared that Nippon will accord independence to the Philippines within this year while independence for Burma "will soon arrive."

He stressed the solidarity of the Greater East Asia Co-Prosperity Sphere and pointed out that China, Manchoukuo, Thailand, Burma, the Philippines, Djawa, Celebes, and other countries in the areas throughout the sphere are extending their utmost cooperation toward Nippon in bringing the current war to a successful end.

KAUGALINGNAN IHATAG SA PILIPINAS NING TUIGA

TOKYO, Hunyo 16 (Domei)—Si Premiyer Tozyo, sa iyang pakigpulong sa atubangan sa Kamara de Pares, sa higayon sa unang pagbukas sa tulo ka adlaw nga gilungtaron sa ika-82 ka tigum nga tinuyo sa Diyeta sukad sa ika-2:00 ang takna karong hapon, nagpahayag nga ang Hapon mohatag ug kaugalingnan sa Pilipinas sulod ning tuiga samtang ang kaugalingnan sa Birmanya (Burma) "umaabut sa labing madali."

Iyang gipasidungog ang panaghiusa sa Lupong sa Pagpauswagay sa Dakudakung Silangan sa Asya ug nagpahayag nga ang Tsina, Mantsukuwo, Tailand, Birmanya, Pilipinas, Djawa, Selebes ug ang ubang mga yuta sulod sa tibuok ginsakupan sa lupong nagahatag sa ilang tugbawng pagbulig ngadto sa Hapon aron pagtapus nga madaugon ning gubata karon.

【東京十六日發同盟】東條首相は十六日午後の臨時議會施政演説において本年中に比島

本年中に比島獨立許容

東條首相、議會で聲明す

に獨立を許容する旨言明した

外號

昭和十八年六月六日
十六日後午後六時
發行

This flyer was handed out to the Filipinos in June, 1943, notifying them of their coming "independence." The information was transmitted in English, Tagalog, Chinese, and Japanese.

more. A West Point man with your potential should think more about the odds." I had other plans developing which I thought were better and with more of a chance to succeed. We parted with an agreement to think the plan over and to talk more later.

A few weeks later, at the evening meal just before sundown, I was sitting in front of my barracks, which was right across from the mess hall, eating my rice. All of a sudden there was a loud yell from the camp gate, and I could see two people struggling. Immediately I recognized that one of the men was a Jap guard and the other was Charlie. The distance wasn't more than 75 yards.

They continued to wrestle and I could see that Charlie had not succeeded in getting the guard's rifle. The guard yelled at the top of his voice. Quickly some other Japs showed up and threw Charlie down. A Jap officer arrived and I could see him trying to talk to Charlie who was surrounded by guards and held by the arms. Several of the guards struck at his legs with their rifle butts. Charlie hadn't uttered a sound that I could hear.

Shortly afterward, the Japanese marched him off down the road to the guard house. By this time it was dark. They must have tied him up in the guard house. We could hear him screaming throughout the night. We felt so helpless, but there was nothing we could do. We never saw Charlie again.

We understood that they had taken him off the next morning and shot him. The Japanese announced that he had died of his wounds received in his escape attempt!

The work details went on. I went back to work on the rice mill detail again. The harvested rice from the paddies was brought to the mill in large baskets on the narrow-gauge train. The detail began early, at dawn. We marched to the mill, about a kilometer away, carrying our mess kits with steamed rice for lunch. The detail was broken up into groups. Different groups unloaded the rice baskets, spread the rice on the bamboo mats in the sun. The rice on the mats had to be turned constantly with bamboo rakes which we used to push the rice back and forth on the mat. It took two days for the rice to dry and to be ready for the dehusking machines.

The bamboo mats were kept rolled up in the warehouse when not in use. They measured 10 or 15 feet long and 10 feet wide – larger than a room-sized rug. We had to get the mats, carry them outside, and unroll them on the ground. They were always full of insects: scorpions and ants, mostly scorpions. This gave me an idea: Why not catch scorpions and somehow put them in the guards' clothes?

In the afternoon before going back to their barracks, the guards would always take a shower at the mill. They hung their clothes on a line outside the shower hut. I collected a match box full of scorpions and found a chance one day to dump them in a pair of pants on the line. We had to go back to camp before the Japanese finished showering, but I'm sure one of the guards missed work for a few days.

We had an hour for lunch at the rice mill. The guards would eat their lunch and then take a nap. We would wait until they were asleep, then we would slip off back into the rice mill area which consisted of several galvanized tin buildings which were warehouses. We knew every nook and cranny, and we were continually looking for something we could eat, use, or take advantage of.

After the dried kernals were put through the dehusking machines, the rice was loaded into 50-kilo sacks which we then had to carry to the storage bodega where it was stacked awaiting shipment to Davao. At times we made a contest out of carrying the sacks to the warehouse, about a 30-yard walk. Anything to break the monotony of doing the same thing day after day. We would see who could carry the most bags at one time.

Some of the men could carry three sacks at a time, urged on by both guards and the other prisoners. The best I did was two sacks at a time. I wonder if that, plus carrying those heavy kapok logs on the fence detail, contributed to my later back problems. After all, two bags of rice weighed more than 220 pounds and my weight was down to about 140 pounds!

Another diversion was killing rats. The rice mill was overrun with rats. They hid behind or under everything. From time to time, after we had stored all the rice bags for that day, the guards would let us hunt rats. Working together, several of us would move the bags while others stood by with good-sized sticks. As the rats ran out, we would dash around wildly, trying to kill as many as possible. It was just another diversion and we had some fun.

I'm sure we didn't make a dent in the rat population and, although we would eat just about anything, we drew the line at rats, even though they are regularly eaten in parts of the Philippines, Thailand, Viet Nam, and Indonesia.

One of the jobs at the rice mill was to feed the fish in a pond about half a kilometer away. Two to four men, with large bamboo baskets three to four feet wide and two feet deep on poles between them, gathered kangkong from the ditches around the rice mill and filled the baskets. These we carried to the fish pond in an isolated area on the other side of the camp. We chopped up the kangkong with bolos which were issued to us, and scattered it on the water for the fish to eat. The fish were grass carp which, when fat, went to the Japanese mess. We never got any of them.

This detail was a good one. We didn't get any fish, but we passed jackfruit trees on the way to the pond. These fruits are delicious when ripe. The large football-sized fruit grow on a small to medium-sized tree. The fruit has large seeds covered with a gelantinous meat. The meat tastes like banana oil smells and is delicious. We saved the large seeds because we could roast them. They were about the size and texture of a Brazil nut. Besides food, this detail offered real possibility of escape. My spirits soared with the hope of freedom.

Since I had blown my chance of escaping with my friend, the Filipino convict, I had continued to think about escaping from the rice mill in spite of the unhappy event of Charlie's disastrous attempt. At this time I was planning with another first lieutenant on the rice mill detail. We began to store away extra rice in the mill as well as two bolos. We pried up a couple of boards in the floor of one of the warehouses and, under these, we stashed our provisions, bolos, and rope.

Over the period of several weeks we had pretty well established that we were to be picked for the fish feeding detail. The fish were in an isolated area, near the edge of the jungle, and we had only one guard with a rifle. We were going to hide our bolos, extra rice, rope, and any other supplies under the kangkong in the baskets that we carried to the fish pond. Once there, we were going to kill the guard and head for the jungle. By traveling north or northeast from the area, we would be in sparsely populated country and hoped to contact friendly Filipino resistance groups in a day or so.

We continued at the rice mill and our escape plans were ready. We were going to make our move in the next day or so. Whenever we talked together, we tried to get off by ourselves during the noon lunch break. We were finally ready to go the next day. That evening when I got back to camp and after the evening meal, I got word that Colonel Olson, the U.S. camp commander, wanted to see me. I went up the the barracks where the colonel had his headquarters. He wasted no time.

"Lieutenant Wills, I understand that you are planning to escape. I know you have hidden away supplies at the rice mill; this can cause very serious trouble for the camp and maybe even death for some of the other prisoners. I have to take steps to prevent this from happening so I am confining you to the POW compound. You are not going out on any more work details."

I didn't bother to argue that I considered it my duty to try to escape to rejoin our forces. During the conversation I said almost nothing except "yes, sir," and "no, sir." I didn't even admit to stashing away supplies, but I did take a distinct dislike to Colonel Olson. He knew as well as I did that the Japanese were no longer making reprisal executions for anyone escaping. The only death possibly resulting would be my own. Colonel Olson was one of those prisoners who thought if they didn't do anything to rock the boat, they would survive to go home. They didn't even consider that the duty of a soldier was to escape.

My chance to escape was gone, but I still planned that there would be another time. I never found out who had overheard our conversations and reported to Colonel Olson, but I didn't rule out the first lieutenant who acted like he was interested in escaping with me. I noticed that he was not confined to camp. Anyway, I began to realize that I would have to make my try alone.

I couldn't stay idle, so I had to look for work inside the compound. I volunteered to repair books in our "library." The old books that we had been given were mostly in very bad shape. So I became a bookbinder. I took off the hard covers, sewed the pages together with abaca fiber thread, mixed up rice paste, and then glued the covers back on. This detail went on for a number of weeks, and while I was getting the smallest rice ration, at least the job kept me busy and not feeling sorry for myself.

Late in March, 1944, there was a big commotion in the farm area. We wondered what had happened. Later we heard that someone on a detail had gone crazy. He had attacked and killed a guard. Others on the detail had escaped into the jungle. The guards had caught one man and had shot him, a chief petty officer named Boone from the Navy. He was frail, not in good health, and evidently couldn't keep up with the others who got away.

Again, as a result of the escape, our rice ration was cut. I needed to quan food more than ever, but there wasn't much of a chance inside the compound, so I just bided my time. The work details resumed and over the next few weeks life in camp went on as before.

By this time it was apparent that on the skimpy diet we were receiving, we were eventually going to starve to death. Our rice ration had been reduced and in spite of the great quantity of vegetables and fruit being grown at the colony, we were getting very little of it. The many tropical fruits in the orchards were allowed to rot on the ground rather than being given to the POWs. In a land of plenty we were systematically being starved to death. There was no other reason for the Japanese refusing to let us harvest the unused produce.

In the spring of 1944, to celebrate the Emperor's birthday, the Japs distributed some Red Cross packages that they had been holding for a long time. They also gave out bananas, assorted fruits, and some meat for the mess hall. We enjoyed the goodies from the Red Cross packages. They were a godsend at this time of severely reduced rations. I put aside some more chocolate and crackers in an escape package together with my burning glass and the compass that I had been able to hide all of this time in prison. Of course, I still had my medicines in a small can and a couple of bottles.

Our news of the outside world was still nil. We only heard occasional rumors of guerrilla actions in Mindanao and we had no idea of where or how numerous these guerrillas might be. Some of us just had the feeling that the Filipino people were resisting the Japanese and we would contact these groups if we could just get out of prison.

Not long after came the news that we were to be moved – to another camp or to Japan. I resolved I would not go to Japan. In early June I was on shipboard, rounding Zamboanga . . .

5. Contact with Guerrillas

I CAME out of my daze – induced by the long desperate swim, the terrible mosquitoes, the stinging nettles, and my sharp memories of imprisonment – and became aware of my surroundings again. I was still sitting in the bushes in my little clearing on the hillside. It must have been about noon since the sun was high and it was getting hot.

There was no sign of anyone. I knew there were people in the vicinity, however, because of the fires I had seen at night. After waiting a while longer, I decided to walk down the beach to see what I could find. Before starting, I took a good drink in the creek and ate half a chocolate bar from the socks around my middle. I broke off a stick about five feet long from a dead tree. I planned to use this as a club. It would be my only weapon.

Just as I was ready to start exploring, I discovered definite signs that someone had been in the vicinity fairly recently. Under a big tree in the bushes near the stream, I found a half completed *banca*, or canoe. Someone had cut a big log and was hollowing it out. I also discovered several paths leading away from the beach.

With some apprehension I started walking south along one of the paths, very carefully looking ahead around every turn and over every hill. I knew that the Japanese had put a price on the capture of any American.

There were cliffs along the shore, and the path cut inland and led over the tops of them. Sometimes the path led through the jungle, sometimes through the cogon grass fields, and at other times, I was walking along the sandy beach. I forded several small streams, walking south along the west coast of Zamboanga. It was a beautiful clear, sunny day and although I was free, I realized that I was a long way from safe. I had to find friendly natives or live in the jungle. I now had realized that I didn't even have a knife. I did have medicine, my compass, and a magnifying glass to start a fire. I proceeded cautiously, being sure that I would see anyone before they saw me.

I had walked for about an hour when the path led out of the jungle onto the beach beside a large stream. Across the stream, which was almost a river, and about five hundred yards away, I saw some smoke coming from a small nipa shack. In front of the shack two women with some small children and three men had gathered. They had not seen me, so I stayed back in the bushes to watch for awhile. They were obviously preparing breakfast. From their appearance, I decided that they were alone, no Japanese were around. At least I didn't see any signs of them.

The natives wore crudely made clothes of abaca, dyed black. The men wore loose Moro pants, and the women wore the Moro *patajong*, or sarong. The men carried *barongs*, large Moro-type knives. No boats were tied up or pulled up on the bank of the stream or on the beach.

After a short while I stepped out on the beach beside the stream and called out to them. As soon as they saw me, the women and children and one man disappeared into the jungle. The other two men just stood and waited. I started wading across the stream which became shoulder deep. Then I walked up into the shallows on the other side, out onto the beach and toward them. When I was about ten yards away, one of the men reached for his barong. I stopped. I decided that I must be an unusual looking sight – a white man, wearing only underwear and a torn tee shirt, skin covered with red blotches, hair matted, beard scruffy, and carrying a small bundle of two socks and a big stick.

I dropped the stick to show them that I didn't intend to fight. Then I said "hello" and smiled. I spoke in English, of course, which they could not understand. But my act and smile must have seemed friendly. One man let go of his barong and they both moved closer, although they still didn't smile. I tried talking in English and in the little bit of Spanish and Tagalog that I knew, but they didn't understand. We sat down and I tried sign language and pictures in the sand, without much success. They talked among themselves and once or twice I caught the word, "hapon." I knew that the word meant "Japanese" in at least several different Filipino dialects. I thought that they were debating whether or not to turn me over to the Japanese.

I decided to get away from there as quickly as possible. Just as I stood up and was getting ready to leave, one of the men called toward the jungle. The women and the children came down to the beach bringing some roasted green bananas which they offered to me. With this, things looked better. I sat down to eat those bananas with relish, but I still wondered where the other man had gone. The fact that the women and children had come out of hiding indicated that the tension was off.

I later learned that in using the word "hapon," they were talking about the shooting during the night when I had escaped and not about the Japanese. I had mistaken the word "hapun," meaning "night" for the word "hapon," meaning Japanese. These people were very primitive and I couldn't make them understand much of anything. We just sat there eating roasted bananas while they kept grinning and nodding their heads once in a while at my sand pictures and signs. Probably they had never seen a white man before. They were, as I learned later, members of a Kolunbugan Moro tribe living in the vicinity.

The Joloano, Kolumbugan, and Sadjug Moros who inhabit the seldom-visited fishing villages of the Zamboanga west coast originally migrated there from the Sulu Archipeligo. Ranging north in their sea-going *vintas*, they chose this lush, verdant coast as their new home. Here they are essentially the same as their brothers to the south in Sulu, Jolo, Tawi Tawi, and Palawan, but their customs and way of life have become modified, simplified, and more primitive.

This part of the western coast of Zamboanga, from its southern tip at Zamboanga City and north for about 125 miles, is very sparsely populated and relatively unexplored. The inhabitants live in small fishing villages and are small groups of Moros who belong to the sea gypsy branch of Moros called Sadjug Moros, or they are Subanos, another tribe indigenous to the area. There are mountain Subanos and coastal Subanos. These people with whom I was trying desperately to talk belonged to one of those groups.

Somewhat later the missing man returned with a banca, and although I couldn't find out where he had been, he seemed a little bit more intelligent. I asked him for "Americano." He smiled and indicated that I was to go with him. Before we left, I made sure the woman gave two quinine tablets to one of the babies who appeared to have malaria. I also gave each one of them a small piece of chocolate. These acts seemed to impress them quite a bit. When we parted, we were already good friends.

Both of the men and I got into the banca, and we started paddling down the coast. We traveled about two hours until we came to a Moro settlement of two houses in a coconut grove set back from the beach a short distance. Some children and a few men were standing around when we arrived. My guides led me to the largest house, a long narrow affair about thirty by twenty feet with a high peaked roof made of palm leaves. I didn't know it then, but we were at the Moro settlement of Panganuran.

The house, built on poles eight or nine feet off the ground, could be entered only by climbing a notched coconut log that could be pulled up into the house at night. The house, built of bamboo and woven nipa palm sides, had flooring of split bamboo. Several of these houses of different sizes filled the clearing. The inside of this house was rather bare. A stove near the door consisted of a couple of earthenware pots sitting in a box of dirt or earth. The only sleeping platform was a raised section of the floor at the far end of the house. Slits in the wall served as the only windows. Pots, spears, rattan fish traps, dried meat, bananas and miscellaneous articles of clothing hung from the rafters and were covered with a deep deposit of soot. Under the house rattan cages held a few chickens and a couple of young pigs.

A man, whom I took to be the chief or *datu*, was sitting on the raised platform at the other end of the house. He made no attempt to greet me. I began to get the feeling that I hadn't made too much of an impression as to my importance, and I wasn't surprised when I thought about how I looked: a skinny, emaciated white man in a pair of baggy underwear pants, torn tee shirt, without shoes, and in my hands a couple of socks tied together.

A couple of women were cooking some fish when I arrived. They put down a grass mat by the fireplace and indicated that I could lie down. They also opened a couple of green coconuts for me, but they still didn't offer me any of the fish, which looked pretty good, especially to a man who hadn't eaten much in two days.

While I was eating the coconuts, a Moro pundit or priest arrived and tried to talk to me. Neither of us could understand the other, however, and he soon gave up in obvious disgust. He apparently pointed out to the others that I was a nobody. I was sure then that I wouldn't be treated too well. Still, no one had made any threatening moves, and I considered myself safe, at least for the time being.

During the afternoon I took out my compass and laid it in the sun to dry along with the bottles of medicine. Several of them had leaked and some of the pills were wet. The people were very interested in this procedure, but they did not make any attempt to take away anything, although several of them tried to find out what they were. The people were having some kind of religious service most of the afternoon. I watched that from a safe, noncommittal distance. The women were all dressed up in their patajongs. There was a beating of brass gongs and bamboo sticks. This went on for quite some time and was quite interesting. I wished that I could understand what they were doing. The day wore on. It was peaceful in the little village, but I was beginning to wonder how long this would go on and how it was going to turn out for me. Everyone just ignored me. I began to wonder if the datu, who didn't pay any attention to me, was considering sending out word to a Jap garrison that he had an American for which there was no doubt a reward. I considered the possibility that I would leave if things didn't look better and go hide in the jungle.

Later in the afternoon, I went back to the house and this time, the women offered me some rice and dried fish in a coconut bowl. I was very busy eating this with my fingers and savoring every morsel, using the first two fingers of my right hand with my thumb, in the typical native Filipino way of eating rice, when all of a sudden I heard a commotion outside. I got up, walked over to the door, looked out, and was startled to see two men just arrive in the clearing. They both carried rifles. For a moment I thought they were Japanese militia. They were dressed like the other Moros in loose pants and the woven bamboo hats. However, I knew almost instantly that they were friendly guerrillas, and I called out to them. They were amazed to see a white man standing in the door, even though I was dressed in underwear, and they lost no time in running over and climbing up the pole into the house.

I identified myself to the two Moro soldiers by showing them my Army ID tags, and they immediately were impressed that I was a first lieutenant in the United States Army. A few words passed between them and the Moro datu, and I began to get more attention than I had commanded before. Some ripe bananas were brought out, a fresh fish was located, and the women began to bake it. We sat around eating the bananas, fish, and some rice, discussing various things about the guerrillas, the American army, and my escape.

They spoke English pretty well and immediately assured me that they were members of a guerrilla unit with its headquarters down the coast. I was elated. I had contacted friendly guerrillas and my escape plan was on schedule. One more hurdle had been cleared. They were two Moros whose names were Sali Abdurazid and Abdul Suliman. I will never forget those names of the first two friendly guerrillas that I met. They had been educated in school in Zamboanga, where they had lived before the war. After the surrender of the Philippines, they left town and joined the guerrillas in the hills. They had just come down from headquarters in northern Zamboanga and were going back to their company headquarters at Siokon, a Moro barrio about 90 kilometers down the coast. They insisted that I go there with them to meet their commander, who, they said, was a Filipino mestizo, Lt. Albert Johnston. They told me a bit about the guerrilla organization. This certainly sounded good. This was what I had been hoping for. My calculated risk of escape had paid off. Now things were going to be different. Although it was still a long, long walk to contact the guerrilla units on the other side of the peninsula, I knew I could make that, and I intended to stay around and settle a few scores with the Japanese.

The two guerrillas talked the Moro datu into lending us one of this vintas, which is a Moro sailboat, and we decided to leave early that night. They said the trip would take about 24 hours, if the wind was good. We thanked the Moro datu for everything and shoved off at about dark. Our boat was an outrigger with two bamboo outriggers on each side. It was about 20 feet long with a sail made of woven mats. The hull was narrow, long and slim, approximately two and a half to three feet wide. In the center was a built-up platform of split bamboo which made an area in which to sit, sleep, or eat. It was a fine night for sailing, with moderate breeze and no waves. I was a bit worried about being picked up by Japanese launches, but the two soldiers assured me they would stay close to the shore and pull in and hide if a launch was sighted. Sali told me there were no Japanese posted on this coast, but they patrolled once in a while with launches and sometimes stopped at the fishing village to get coconuts or to take fish away from the natives. They told me that the Japanese had bombed and strafed Siokon, where the company was located, about three weeks ago. The bombing had caused a couple of houses to burn, but no one had been hurt.

As we sailed down the coast, the weather was so perfect and enjoyable that I lay down on the bamboo platform and listened to the water hissing by the hull and watched the shoreline slip by. Sali and Abdul were doing all the work. The phosphorescence of the water streamed out behind us and except for the sound of the boat and the ocean, it was very peaceful. We traveled all night and in the morning put into shore to get some coconut milk to drink at a place called Pitamis, a small Moro settlement. Wild coconut palms grew all along the coast. We beached the boat, walked over, and one of the boys climbed a tree and shook a few coconuts down. We then had plenty to eat and drink. We shoved off again and traveled the rest of the day, arriving at Dicolum, a Moro fishing village about four o'clock in the afternoon. We stayed overnight with a Filipino named Logan Johnston who had fled from Zamboango when the Japanese came and who was living in this isolated place with his wife. Logan was not in good health but agreed to go with us the next day to Siokon where his brother Albert was commander of the guerrilla unit there. The next morning we sailed down the coast to Baligian, a Moro fishing village.

When we landed, crowds of people gathered around to watch us and I felt rather foolish in underwear shorts, especially when the girls got together and giggled at the funny-looking white man. The people were typical Joloano Moros. The men wore loose, baggy trousers, head cloths, and short jackets which buttoned up the front. They carried barongs or krisses, and they were all chewing betelnut and wore metal betelnut boxes tied around their waists with woven rope. The women wore *mailongs,* which are something like sarongs. They also wore long jackets decorated with gold and silver buttons, most made from coins. Even though it was a very poor, primitive fishing village, the people were friendly and offered us coffee, fried bananas, tobacco, betelnut. In fact, anything we wanted. Evidently they had seldom seen a white man, if ever. I met the datu, whose name was Salila, and he insisted on presenting me with a metal betel box in its rope-carrying belt. Later on I would use it to carry some of my medicine.

We rested for about an hour. While I ate fried bananas, Sali and Abdul told the people my story. We finally got away and walked inland the four kilometers to Siokon. We arrived about dark and located Albert Johnston in a two-story house where he made his headquarters. He was amazed to see a white man with the two soldiers, but he was also overjoyed and immediately called in all of his company officers and introduced me to them. They had all been in the Philippine army before the surrender. Most of them were still wearing their insignia, although none of them had complete uniforms. Some had a khaki shirt, others khaki pants, others were dressed in typical Moro gear. Most of them were barefooted or wearing Moro sandals. I felt self-conscious in my underwear pants and T shirt, but I already had my betel box tied around my waist.

WAR DEPARTMENT

THE ADJUTANT GENERAL'S OFFICE

WASHINGTON 25, D. C.

HJR/jts

IN REPLY REFER TO:
AGPO-C 201 Wills, Donald H.
(14 Nov 44) 319116-S-7
0389373

18 November 1944.

Mr. Charles H. Wills,
198 Huron Avenue,
Lynchburg, Virginia.

Dear Mr. Wills:

It is a pleasure to inform you that your son, First Lieutenant Donald H. Wills, 0389373, has been reported from a reliable but
unofficial source to have escaped from enemy hands and to be safe with
guerilla forces. No other information has been received since the letter
from this office of 30 December 1942, but you may be certain that any
additional reports will be forwarded to you promptly upon receipt.

This notification of your son's safety is given to you in
confidence with the request that it be disclosed to no one outside of
your immediate family as it is most important that no publicity whatever be given to this information. This precaution is necessary in the
best interest of our country and any deviation from strict confidence
might jeopardize the safety of your son and of other personnel.

Sincerely yours,

Robert H. Dunlop

ROBERT H. DUNLOP,
Brigadier General,
Acting The Adjutant General.

**This letter, received by my parents from the War Department, brought the good
news that I had escaped and was safe. Good news travels slowly. It took from
June to November, 1944, for my parents to learn of my escape.**

Johnston and I went about a half kilometer farther inland to a house
where his wife was staying with the family of another lieutenant. The house
was a large two-story frame building. They gave me a room upstairs and insisted I stay there with them. Mrs. Johnston gave me a cotton blanket, a
mosquito net, and a very-much-appreciated khaki shirt and a pair of khaki
pants. Luckily, I had lost considerable weight. I was down to about 125
pounds, and they fitted me. I still had no shoes.

Before the war, Johnston and his brothers, who were also hiding in the

Opposite: My betel box on its rope belt, with the original containers of medicine
that I escaped with and also my escape compass and head cloth given by *Datu*
Salila.

hills, had owned a large lumber mill in Zamboanga City. They had been taken prisoner by the Japanese after the surrender of Mindanao, but had escaped after a short time. Albert, commanding officer of G. Company at Siokon, which was a lumber camp owned by his family, had about 75 men under him. Because of sickness and special details to higher headquarters, he only had about 30 men for duty. At that time their military equipment was somewhat limited. They had only 15 rifles for the 30 men. They had no radio, and all communication was sent by runner. The division headquarters was 10 days away up the coast of Zamboanga. Colonel Bowler's headquarters, which was over in A Corps on the other side of the peninsula in Misamis, was 16 days' hike away. Johnston immediately sent a runner to notify those at headquarters of my arrival.

I was quite thin and my feet were cut badly from walking barefooted since I had come ashore, so I decided to rest in Siokon before reporting to Colonel Bowler in A Corps. In addition to sore feet, I was still having some trouble with malaria. I stayed in Siokon for three weeks, and during that time I gained 15 pounds. I would have gained more because the food was certainly very good after prison fare, but I had two attacks of malaria and the quinine I was taking killed my appetite somewhat. I thought this was a good time to see if I could get rid of malaria, so over a period of the two or three weeks, I took a complete course of quinine, consisting of 30 grains a day, enough to make my head buzz and ring all the time. After finishing that course, I took a course of plasmacin, which was a specific drug at that time for another type of malaria. I also took a course of atabrine. After these courses, I never again in my life had another malaria attack. The cut on my wrist was healing nicely and my ears had stopped aching.

Johnston did his best to show me around the country and told me a lot about the guerrilla organization. Actually, the mission of his unit was to maintain the esprit de corps among the native Filipinos who were not cooperating with the Japanese. In such an isolated position and having no means of communication, about the only thing his unit could do was to shoot at and harass the Japanese patrol boats as they moved along the coast. That is why the Japs had bombed his headquarters a short time ago. I later learned that there were many of these isolated guerrilla units spotted around various inaccessible parts of the Philippines. They were just another part of the resistance of the Filipino people against the Japanese. As the guerrillas became more organized and received more supplies through delivery by air drops or by submarine, these units then carried out coast watcher duties and more active harassment against the Jap patrols, and contributed to the general intelligence of Japanese movements and actions on the island.

6. Life with the Guerrillas in the Hills

EVERYTHING that they had at Siokon had to be improvised from materials available. During the short time I stayed with them, I learned about how the natives live off the land and how guerrillas live with practically no support from the outside world. Of course, we were living in a tropical area, roughly five degrees off the equator, and in such a lush, tropical climate, it was almost easy to live off the country. With coconut, bamboo, palm, and palmetto trees, and the different tubers available along the streams and small lakes and with the sea nearby, it was possible to get everything needed to live. It was a fascinating lesson in survival, living off the countryside, and in the coming weeks, I learned many things that would help me in later situations.

If a person on a tropical island had a few clumps of bamboo and a bunch of coconut trees, he could get along very well. He could almost exist without drinking water. Take the coconut, for instance. The coconut tree can be used to make a shelter with palm leaves for the roof. They can also be used for any number of things such as walls of the house, baskets, and hats. The husk taken off the outside of the coconut furnished firewood if you don't have anything else to burn. After burning it, you can leach the ashes to get lye. The coconut can be cracked open and can be gathered green or ripe. If green, they have to be pulled off the tree. It they are ripened, most of them will fall to the ground or you can knock them down. The green coconut, except for extracting the drinking water out of it, is usually not as good for a food supply. The unmatured meat inside is a jelly-like consistency but very pleasant to eat.

After breaking open the ripe coconut, you have anywhere from a quarter to one half an inch thickness of coconut meat. It is white, dense material very high in oil (about 68 percent). You can eat it like it is or grate it and then knead it with water, making coconut milk, which is actually an emulsion of the oil in water. You can use it in place of milk if you have cereal. They didn't have cereal, but would take a certain type of glutenous rice and pound it flat in a pestle made out of a coconut log. The rice could be toasted or popped, then sweetened with sugar-cane syrup and eaten with the coconut milk. You could dry the coconut meat in the sun or over a fire and then extract the oil. The women shaved the coconut meat into thin slivers, threw it into an old 55-gallon drum with water, and boiled it until the oil separated and floated to the top. Then they had a nice clear oil for cooking, for lamps, or for anything else which oil could be used for. The meal from the coconut meat after the oil is extracted is around 8 or 9 percent protein and was fed to carabao or cows.

Then the bamboo. From eating Chinese food everyone knows about bamboo shoots. In the tropics nearly any time of the year there will be bamboo shoots pushing up through the ground around the bamboo trees. A peculiarity of bamboo is that the size of the shoot that pushes up through the ground and eventually develops into a stalk of bamboo determines the size of the stalk. You have bamboo up to three or four inches in diameter, so it was common to get bamboo shoots which were three or four inches in diameter. After peeling off the outside rough husk, the Filipinos boil them in water twice to remove the bitterness. Sliced, bamboo shoots make a succulent vegetable. Of course, the bamboo contributed much to building materials. The stalks were split and flattened out, woven together and made into mats, walls, or flooring. Bamboo could also be bound with rattan vines from the jungle to make masts for boats, or rafters for a house. The stalks could be split with the sections on the inside removed and used for gutters and pipes for water. Again, the bamboo could be burned for fuel and the ashes could be leached for lye. Then the coconut oil and the lye could be used to produce soap, a very good soap which makes suds in sea water.

Coconut oil can be burned in a diesel engine, which we did many times. The two diesel engines at Siokon we ran on coconut oil by heating the heads of the engines. Once we got them hot they ran perfectly well on the oil. In addition, the young shoots of the coconut flower stalk that grows out of the top of the tree produce a sap. Bind those flower stalks together, bend them over, cut off the end, and hang a bucket over the end. The sap can be collected overnight. Each morning, two or three quarts of sap will have collected. Then the cut was renewed on the flower stalk and the process repeated the next morning.

The sap has a taste like sweet cidar. If it is allowed to ferment, then by the night or perhaps the next day, it tasted somewhat like wine. Four or five glasses of *tuba*, the fermented drink, produced a good buzz. Obviously, if you let it continue to ferment, it would turn into vinegar, which could be used for cooking. Or the tuba could be used before it turned to vinegar by adding sugar cane, boiling it in 55-gallon drums, and double distilling it, producing an alcohol that would run an automobile engine if you enlarged the carburetor jets. This we did. We didn't have automobiles in Siokon, but later, on the other side of the island, we ran many autos using alcohol. Then, by distilling the crude alcohol three times, we had medical alcohol for use in the hospitals or for a drink of about 150 proof.

Incidentally, oil from the coconuts made a very good light. We poured it into a seashell or an open can with cotton or fabric wick. Lighted, it was a nice, almost smokeless light, which was about the only light we had in Siokon.

Sections of bamboo could be made into utensils or food containers or water containers of various kinds. The Subanos and the Moros used long sections of bamboo, perhaps five or six feet long and four or five inches in diameter, with the interior sections knocked out. By cutting a hole in the side, they could fill this with water and carry water from the streams to be stored in their houses. Coconut shells made containers and bowls of all kinds. We usually ate from coconut shell bowls. Spoons could be fashioned from coconut shells.

In the inland valleys around Siokon, the natives grew a lot of rice which was the staple food in their diet. There were a number of tubers available like *gabi*, which was an elephant-ear type of leaf that grew near the streams. Its root stock was a starchy, edible vegetable much like a potato. Casaba root could be made into tapioca or just eaten roasted. Some corn was grown also.

In addition to *pomalos,* which are like a grapefruit, we had limes as big as baseballs, some oranges (not quite as good as those in the States), bananas of all kinds (wild, cultivated, small bananas the size of your thumb to big plantains two inches in diameter and a foot long). We ate red, yellow, or green bananas. The green bananas were cooking bananas and were boiled or fried. We also feasted on mangos, guavas, guabanos, breadfruit (a large basketball-type fruit with spines all over it which was cooked as a starchy food), jack fruit (the kind we "quaned" in prison on the pig detail) and, of course, cashews.

We had *durians* and many tropical fruits like *mangosteens,* found not more than five or six degrees off the equator. In addition, fish abounded along the coast as well as fresh water prawns in the streams. The Filipinos made bamboo baskets and trapped the prawns in the river. These were up to six or eight inches long, similar to shrimp and very good eating. The rice paddies had mud fish in them. With a woven, open-ended bamboo basket, we could spot the bubbles where the mud fish would be. By pushing the basket down over the place where the bubbles appeared, you could reach down through a hole in the top of the basket and find the mud fish with your hand.

We took sap from the breadfruit tree and spread it on twigs in the trees. It was like an adhesive. If the birds landed on it, they couldn't get loose. This way you could catch quite a few birds. As a matter of fact, there were usually a bunch of tame parrots and cockatoos around the various little barrios and fishing villages. They had been caught in just this way.

We had guns and some ammunition and occasionally we shot a wild carabao roaming around in the hills. Some wild cattle also roamed the hills.

These had scattered there since the Japanese had invaded the islands. Back in the mountains, there were wild pigs, so that we occasionally had pork. Food was not a problem in these remote areas.

Clothing was a problem, however. There just wasn't too much of it. The Filipinos used the abaca fibers from the banana-type plant to weave a rough, coarse kind of cloth. They also had some bolt-goods of cotton around. While we didn't have the conventional types of shirts and pants, there were plenty of Moro garments and more than half the time I wore Moro malongs, or loose Moro pants. I usually wore a khaki shirt with a woven bamboo Moro hat, along with Moro slippers or sandals. After acquiring a good sunburn and aside from the light-colored hair, I could have easily passed unnoticed by any patrolling Japanese. My lips, gums, and teeth were not, however, black from betel juice and I didn't have betel juice dripping down the corner of my mouth.

With the application of hot coconut oil and some sulfa, my feet had healed and I could walk anywhere barefooted or in sandals. I guess as the days and weeks passed one might say that I had "gone native." I became well integrated into the Filipino society and I did and acted about like the other Filipinos.

A number of Chinese had evacuated Zamboanga and were living in these remote barrios and fishing villages. The Chinese in the Philippines were usually the small merchants who ran the stores. In the mountains they were still running little shops and always had a small supply of things they got from somewhere.

In June, 1944, Lieutenant Johnston and I were invited to a Chinese merchant's house for dinner. This family managed to come up with a twelve-course meal. I lasted through all twelve, but Johnston dropped out after about eight. This entire banquet took place on the ground floor of a nipa shack with a split bamboo table and benches made out of bamboo sections. In the middle of the table sat a big plate of rice which was passed around with each course. The family started preparing the food when we arrived. They offered us tuba, rice wine, and native cigarettes. While we were sipping wine, smoking, and talking, I noticed that they killed two chickens. Shortly thereafter the first course came through. It was clear chicken soup. I guess they dragged the dead chicken through some boiling water.

This soup was followed shortly by boiled pieces of chicken and then boiled homemade sausage, made from the intestines of pigs and various kinds of meats which were always colored red with the achuete tree seeds. We then were served fried chicken, some bamboo shoots, and some fried sections of eggplant. Eggplant, found in abundance in the tropics, can get as large as two or three inches in diameter and a foot long and sometimes round and as big as a softball. We ate several different kinds of fish in the twelve courses, boiled and fried whole with heads on. We had chunks of fried pork and shredded beef mixed with chopped vegetables. Much of the food I could not identify, but it seemed like a gourmet meal to me.

After the eighth course, the hosts put a plate of bananas on the table. The significance of this was that the bananas had been presented as a sort of dessert. It was then permissible to stop eating. However, they served the other four courses. All during the meal, of course, rice wine and native cigarettes were still available. I was quite impressed that the Chinese did not start preparation of the meal until we arrived and everything was cooked as the meal was going on. In that period of time they came up with all the different food, prepared while we were sitting there eating.

On San Juan Day, June 24, a Catholic holiday, everyone in the Philippines goes on a family picnic. Lieutenant Johnston invited me to go with his wife and their children on a picnic to a nearby swimming hole. Obviously, I accepted. Lieutenant Billantis and his wife and two teenaged daughters, were coming too. One of the daughters, Nanet, was very nice looking. She lived with her parents further inland a couple of kilometers from where I was staying in Siokon. The Billantises lived in a nice, two-story Filipino house. It had several bedrooms, a living room, a separate kitchen, and storage facilities underneath the house. Quite a civilized house, it was situated on the edge of a rice paddy and surrounded by well arranged plantings of flowers and fruit trees. I had become interested in Nanet, so I guess the Johnstons thought I would be a good companion on the picnic.

We were going to have *lechanado*, which is roast pig. Two of Lieutenant Johnston's soldiers came along, carrying the pig on a pole between them. When roasted on the spit over coals, the pig would be the pièce de résistance of the picnic. We walked three kilometers through rice paddies and the fields along the edge of the jungle to a spot on the river where the water was deep enough for swimming and diving. On a flat area along the bank the two soldiers set about building the fire, setting up forked poles, and getting the pig ready for roasting.

We took off our clothes down to our underwear. The girls kept on their slips, and we all went for a swim. The tropical river, too warm to be invigorating, nevertheless felt pleasant after the walk. At first, I felt uneasy. We were quite vulnerable, undressed and unarmed and surrounded by trees and brushy cover which would make slipping up on us quite easy. Lieutenant Johnston assured me that there would be no Japanese or Moro bandits hiding behind trees.

As the pig roasted, and the swimming grew tiresome, Lieutenant Billantis and the soldiers climbed a 20-foot cliff overhanging the river and dived off. This looked like fun to me and, not to be outdone, I climbed up and pushed off, straightening into a graceful dive which nearly resulted in disaster. My dive was not shallow as the other dives had been, and I plowed into the bottom. When I came up, most of the skin on one side of my face

Cooking *lechanado* (suckling pig roasted over coals) the Filipino way.

from my forehead to my chin was scraped off. In my carelessness in not testing the depth before diving, I came close to breaking my neck. I had a stiff neck for a long time. After my long imprisonment and my taste of freedom after my harrowing escape, I had nearly thrown it all away by being careless. I made a mental vow to be more cautious and to live to join the main guerrilla forces on the other side of Mindanao. I wanted desperately to get back into the fight again.

The swimming and diving made us hungry. The roast pig smelled delicious. We stood around in our wet clothes, pulling off bits of charred skin (cracklings) and the succulent, tender meat underneath. We washed it down with plenty of cool tuba brought in hollowed-out bamboo sections. With Nanet there, I had a splendid time. I had seen so few women for the past several years that all of the girls at Siokon looked attractive, but Nanet more so than the others. She was somewhat larger than the average Filipino woman and must have been around 18 or 20. She had light skin, long jet black hair, and a well developed figure. Nanet was easier to talk to than the other girls, who were generally pretty shy, at least around me. Our conversation, however, was mostly one sided, with me asking all about Filipino customs and way of life. Nanet willingly answered my questions and explained about life in Siokon. She attended school in Zamboanga before the war and spoke good English.

Later in the afternoon we walked back through the rice paddies. Over a couple of glasses of tuba and by the light of a coconut oil lamp, Nanet and I talked until late in the evening. It wasn't a private conversation, young kids were running around, in and out of the room, and Mr. and Mrs. Billantis were in evidence and even entered into the conversation from time to time. I think they were encouraging my interest in Nanet. However, I had already decided that I wasn't going to be in Siokon much longer and I didn't want to get into any compromising situation with any women at that time. Also I felt that I must be sure that I had been accepted by the Filipinos as one of them before I risked antagonizing them by making premature passes at any of the women. In the meantime I was enjoying my new-found freedom every minute of the day.

My stellar social experience, however, was yet to come. June is the month of brides in Mindanao, as it is in the States, and in the last of June I was privileged to attend a Moro wedding.

7. A Moro Wedding

LIEUTENANT Johnston and I were invited to a Moro wedding to take place at the bride's house, a bamboo and nipa shack on the beach at Maliput about eight kilometers from Siokon. As the groom was one of our soldiers, Sali Abdurazid, who was marrying a winsome girl, Sibulan, it was imperative that we attend. If we did not go, the couple would be insulted. To look properly important and to add prestige to the wedding, Johnston and I each took along two armed bodyguards. If we had gone without them, we probably would have lost face. The wedding was in the afternoon and the ceremony was not to begin until our arrival, so we planned to arrive early.

The eight-kilometer walk followed logging roads and wound through the rice paddies along the edge of the jungle. At one place the trail followed a log bridge almost a mile long over a crocodile-infested swamp. The bridge was made up of logs laid down end to end and supported on posts driven into the swamp. Johnston cautioned me that on the return trip, we must be sure to cross this swamp before dark. I agreed with him fully, as I didn't like the idea of slipping off one of those round logs in the dark with crocodiles everywhere in the swamp. Crossing in the daytime with wet, bare feet was trouble enough. The Filipinos could walk along nonchalantly as if on a flat pathway, but I wasn't that good. I had to inch along using my arms as a balance.

Later that morning when we arrived at the house, most of the people had gathered and were waiting for us. The house, nestled in a clump of coconut trees, was about twenty yards back from the beach. Made of split bamboo with a cogon grass roof, the house consisted of only one large room. Nevertheless, it was more Americanized than most of the shacks in that area for it was only four feet off the ground and instead of a notched pole for access to the house, there were bamboo stairs up to the front door.

For the wedding, the family had constructed two sheds next to the house. These had cogon grass roofs supported by four bamboo poles. One was the cook shed for the guests. Two huge kawas of meat and rice were simmering there. The Moros do not eat pork so the pots contained beef or chicken and fish. Under the other shed, the Moros had built a platform which was two or three feet off the ground and made of split bamboo supported by bamboo logs. I couldn't figure out the use for that platform, but I soon found out.

The crowd consisted of a colorful-looking bunch of Moros. Most of them had never seen a white man or had not seen one for a long time. They crowded around Johnston and me while he told them how I came to be there. To me the people were interesting and, in a way, mysterious. Several Christian Filipinos mingled with the crowd, but the majority of the people were Moros of one kind or another. They were wearing every conceivable type of clothing. The Christian Filipinos dressed in their best, wore slacks and mestizo shirts of embroidered cotton or *piña*, material made of pineapple fiber. The few soldiers present wore nondescript pieces of American clothing mixed with Moro pants and sandals. You could spot them by their guns which they proudly displayed at all times. Moros considered themselves very important people when they had guns!

The Moros wore bright headcloths of red, yellow, and black. Some had on skintight Moro pants and some had loose flowing ones. All were in clashing colors. Stuck into their waistbands were the ever-present daggers or krisses or barongs. All of them had betel boxes either on a rope around their waists or tucked into the tops of their malong or held in their hands. Their blackened teeth were evident between the red-stained lips because they smiled, laughed and shouted while they crowded around to get a better look at the Americano.

As I watched the laughing, smiling faces, it was hard for me to realize that one of these same faces could be that of a *juramantado,* frustrated and contorted with rage, obsessed only with the desire to kill any person not a follower of Islam, especially a white man. Or, one of these men could be one of the band of bandits that had been raiding the Christian towns at Sirawai – only three hours away by vinta. But that's another story, and the wedding was getting under way.

The big kawas over the fire were opened and the people began to collect huge piles of rice and meat on square banana leaves spread around on the ground or on the table under one of the sheds. We were called into the house and given seats of honor on the floor with the groom. We did not have to eat outside, while squatting in the grass. As a courtesy to us, we were served first with coffee and cakes. There were twelve different kinds of cakes. I tried them all, but I got lost in the explanation of how they were made.

One cake was in a shape similar to a pretzel, but it was black. Made from corn kernels slightly charred and then ground into flour, the cake got its color from the "blackened" meal mixed with water and salt. Another type was made from rice flour and brown sugar and was cut into small squares. One was made from dripping rice flour into a pot of boiling coconut oil and collecting a hunk of spaghetti-like fried bread called *locot.* This was tasty when it was hot. Some of the other tasted like nothing more than dough.

We were next served a platter of fried and boiled fish and beef or carabao meat. The carabao, of course, is a water buffalo and is one of the staple meats used by Filipinos. The women had prepared the meat in such a way that it had a greenish color and was very spicy, almost like the curried dishes in some Oriental restaurants in the States. There was plenty of tuba stored in hollow sections of bamboo. This drink was for us. The Moros were forbidden by their religion to drink alcoholic beverages. While we were eating, the people of the household and also the relatives were squatting around on the floor and eating from several dishes of food. No knives or forks were evident. Everyone ate with their fingers, using the first three fingers and the thumb of the right hand. That included Johnston and me and our soldiers. Once you acquire the knack, it's quite easy.

Everyone helped himself from the common bowls of food and we had to be quick or the good pieces would be gone. The fortunate first-comers felt no qualms about picking off the good parts of the fish, and that was always the last third of the fish down near the tail because the big hunks of meat without any bones were there. Anyone who dallied was left with the head and the skeleton to choose from.

All the time that we were eating, the women were preparing the bride for the ceremony. The women of the family and the bride were hidden behind a curtain in the back of the room. No one, except the girls-in-waiting, was supposed to see the bride. Several old crones were on watch for anyone who tried to get a peek. Along with several other Filipinos, I tried to peek through the curtain and was pulled back amid shrieks from the girls behind the curtain. It was all in fun. Everybody laughed and even the old women couldn't hide a smile.

A place for the bride and groom was readied on one side of the room by spreading rugs and mats on the floor. The priest or pundits had arrived with their copies of the Koran, the Islamic bible. Outside, the crowd had finished eating and they repeatedly called upon two of the girls to dance. To the rhythm of clicking bamboo sticks, they had a song duel, each girl taking turns at singing and dancing. The girls performed on the raised platform which earlier had puzzled me as to its use. One girl got up and sang a verse, keeping time to the music with her feet. Then the other one would sing. Each tried to outdo the other. The crowd clapped and yelled when they liked a verse or when the dancing was exceptionally good. However, the crowd seemed more stirred by the words of the songs than by the dancing. The dancers wore the standard Moro mailongs. The dance was similar to some of the Balinese dances which everyone sees on television and on travel posters. The girls use their hands in various positions while stamping and making dance steps with their feet in a kind of slow motion but in rhythm with the clicking bamboo sticks.

The dancing was interrupted by the arrival of Sali, the groom, who was carried on the shoulders of his closest friends. The procession came in from a nearby house, as the groom is not permitted to see the bride on the wedding day before the ceremony. Sali, dressed in his very best, wore a khaki shirt and loose Moro pants with a bright red and black and yellow headcloth. His face was painted chalk white. As part of the ceremony, his friends carried him three times around the house and then brought him in and placed him, sitting, on a pillow. All this time they were kidding him and making jokes, but he, according to custom, had to keep a poker face and show no emotion. Once at some joke he almost smiled, but caught himself in time. The bride had not yet been brought out. The groom sat motionless on his pillow with both of his legs crossed, looking neither to the right nor left. One of the men reached out and straightened his headcloth, but Sali still didn't move.

Finally, the curtains parted and four girls brought out the bride. Seated cross-legged on a pillow, she was motionless. Her face was a mass of white paint. She wore long, four-inch silver fingernails, long gold earrings, and a silver and gold pagoda-like ornament in her hair. She had on a bright green blouse and jacket with gold buttons and a bright mailong of many colors. Of course she was barefooted. Her handmaidens placed her to the right of the groom and, after straightening out her headdress, they retired to squat with the rest of the crowd on the floor in a semicircle surrounding the couple. The Moro priests started to read out of the Koran, taking turns.

The reading went on for quite some time until one of the priests, the highest ranking, I believe, took the hand of the bride and the groom and crossed their thumbs. Holding them thus, he chanted the final words and the ceremony was finished. The bride was taken away by the girls and the groom then relaxed, took off his headcloth, and grabbed something to eat. The bride never reappeared. For the bridegroom, the hardest trial was yet to come. For having been legally married to Sibulan, he must now court her all over again before he could get her to live with him. This probably would take him days or weeks before she would condescend to come to his house, depending upon how he went about the procedure. As we would put it, she was playing "hard to get." He must have gone well though, because he was up at our house a few days later with his bride. She was by then in her everyday clothes. I hardly recognized her as the decorated, white-faced bride I had seen several days earlier. At my wedding present of a few pills of quinine, she smiled shyly, showing pretty white teeth not yet blackened by betelnut. The last I saw of them, several days after the wedding, they were disappearing down the trail back toward the beach. The groom was out in front, followed by the bride, carrying her bundle of extra clothes.

When the ceremony was over in the late afternoon, Lieutenant Johnston and I still had the eight kilometer hike back to Siokon over the crocodile swamp, so we hurried along and managed to cross the swamp before dusk.

We confronted no crocodiles, but it was wild country. The Filipinos were careful about going down to the edge of the rivers or the swamp after dark. If they had to make a trip in a boat or a banca across the river at night, they got into the canoe quickly and did not do much wading around in the water.

When we arrived back at Siokon, the word had come to us that some bandits were causing trouble at Sirawai. Lieutenant Johnston and I decided that we should go there and see what could be done to prevent these raids.

8. Hunting Moro Bandits

BANDITS have always been a problem in the Moro areas of the Philippines and have been especially active in and around the lower Zamboanga Peninsula, the Sulu Archipelago, and around Palawan Island and in the Sulu Sea and Moro Gulf. Raids against Christian settlements and other Moro settlements are not uncommon even today.

After the surrender of the Philippines, the activity of the pirates had increased in these areas, probably due to the absence of any civil action against them. On the southwest coast of Zamboanga in the isolated areas and around Sibuko Bay, Sirawai, and Siokon Bay, the pirates had become quite bold and were raiding settlements on market days, preying on the settlements of refugees who had fled to the areas when the Japanese occupied Zamboanga City.

It was time to send the pirates a message that the raids would not be tolerated so, together with six or eight heavily-armed soldiers, Lieutenant Folisco and I hiked down to the beach and took a vinta down to Sirawai Bay. It was July 1, 1944. The trip took about three hours and, after arriving at Sirawai Bay, we pulled the vinta up on the beach, left the boatman with it, and hiked through the rice paddies, over the grass-covered hills up into the foothills where the Moro bandit village was supposed to be. News travels fast through the "bamboo telegraph," and I felt apprehensive as we approached the village. Everything was quiet, and in this unusual silence even the surrounding jungle was quiet. It occurred to me that hostile bandit Moros might alert the Japanese that they could capture an escaped American at this village. We half expected an ambush which is the Moro way of doing business. Advancing cautiously, we reached the village, a cluster of nipa shacks in a clearing, and we searched house by house. Although we found some spears hidden inside hollow bamboo logs, we didn't find anything else of significance and certainly no people, not even women and children. I had, however, this strange, uneasy feeling that someone watched us as we moved about. After our thorough search, we left and started back to Sirawai.

Later in the afternoon we arrived, and discovered a Moro market was in progress on the beach beside some nipa shacks. Vendors were selling everything from food supplies to brass Moro gongs, and sets of *agongs* and clothes, as well as woven materials of all kinds. Also available for purchase was hardware, knives, handmade knives, and bolos. We looked around the market for an hour or so but didn't buy anything. We made sure that our presence was noticed and that everyone could see that we had plenty of arms and ammunition with us. We put out the word that the bandit attacks would not be tolerated anymore.

After hanging around the market for awhile longer, we went on to visit a Mrs. Bryant, a Filipina who had been married to an American who had been taken into prison camp, so she was living by herself. After spending some time with her, we went on to a Mrs. Holland's house. She also was a Filipina who had married an American who was now being interned in Cebu or somewhere else in the Philippines by the Japanese. She invited us to stay for supper and to spend the night there. We accepted. She lived in a very nicely built house raised up on poles about six or eight feet off the ground. We didn't have to climb up a notched pole, as she had regular wooden stairs. What was significant, however, was that the house was surrounded by a fence of barbed wire about seven feet tall and we came into the yard through a barbed wire gate which was locked behind us. We went into the house which had sides that could be swung out to get air if there was a breeze. Over each one of these openings there was a heavy screen nailed onto the sides of the house so no one could come in or throw anything in for that matter.

We had a very nice supper with Mrs. Holland and then she insisted on bringing out a bunch of old *Popular Mechanics* magazines that her husband had subscribed to. I was able to look at a few of these before the coconut oil lights were out and we went to sleep.

The next day we went on to Labason, which was another barrio up the coast. We went by vinta and stayed in the house of Mr. Angeles and Mrs. Marciana, who was a nurse. We spent the night there and went back to Siokon the next day. We didn't hear, at least while I was in Siokon, which was not too much longer, any more reports of the Moro bandits causing trouble down at Sirawai, so I guess our show of force was worthwhile.

During the time that I stayed at Siokon, from June 16 until July 6, 1944, on several occasions the locals had some dances which they called "bailes." All the local girls would come and the soldiers would show up. The party was somewhat like the old-time country dances in the States. The men lined up along one wall and the women lined up along the other wall. If you wanted to dance with somebody, you had to go over and ask her, then you got out on the floor and danced. Lieutenant Johnston had a five-piece band made up of men from his company who had been in an orchestra in Zamboanga in prewar days. They all had their instruments with them, and the music really sounded pretty good at these dances. Lieutenant Billantis' pretty daughter Nanet came to the dances. I did most of my dancing with her.

On several occasions I went up to see Nanet. After that happened several times, the Filipinos suggested that perhaps I ought to carry out one of the customs that they had. This they called "creeping, creeping." I forget what the word was in Visayan for this, but the object was that if you were real sweet on a girl and thought she liked you, you would see if you could confirm this assumption by abducting her! Obviously, this was a somewhat risky business. Naturally, the girl was sleeping in the house in a separate room from her parents. The "creeper" was supposed to sneak over to her house during the night and by very carefully approaching, you were supposed to get to her bedroom, slip through the window, and abduct her. The custom dictated that if you got as far as her bedroom and into her bedroom and to her bed, and if you could put your hand over her mouth to keep her from yelling, you had already won the game. She would come with you.

Now, depending upon whether she came with you and then later sneaked back into the house or whether you were then stuck and had to get married was something else again that nobody ever explained. I was urged on a number of occasions to carry out a "creeping, creeping" mission against Nanet. I debated it seriously a couple of times but I finally decided that with my position there, having just arrived, and because I was going to leave very shortly, I did not want to cause any ill feeling or commit any cultural faux pas, so I confined my attentions to Nanet by just dancing with her at the dances and on a couple of occasions I went over to her house at night for a date. We sat around and talked, part of the time with the whole family present. We got a chance to go outside and sit on the veranda in the dark, but that's about as far as it went. I didn't think it would be expedient for me to engage in any creeping, creeping campaign. I was going to be around in Mindanao for some time and my chief goal was to join the main group of guerrillas and be ready for the fight to liberate the island.

Because the Filipinos asked me if I was interested indicated to me that I was well accepted into their society. By this time I was beginning to pick up a few of the Visayan words, and I could understand quite a bit when they were talking in their dialect, but I wasn't fluent by any means. Traveling around, visiting the Moro barrios, learning the customs of the rural Filipinos, provided for me in the three weeks that I spent in Siokon with Johnston and his soldiers one of the most informative, interesting, and enjoyable times in Mindanao. I could eat fish and rice three times a day, I could even eat the salted, half-rotten fish called *ginamus* (Filipino caviar) and enjoy them all. In fact there wasn't anything I couldn't eat. Of course, all of this might have been colored by the fact that I had come directly out of prison camp and everything seemed so great after the conditions in the Japanese prison.

The cuts on my feet had long since healed, and the soles were tough enough so that I could walk almost anywhere the Filipinos could. We walked eight to ten kilometers at a stretch over rice dikes, gravel beaches, jungle trails, thinking nothing of it. I had gained a lot of weight back, and I felt fine. By this time, I was getting impatient to go north and report to Colonel Bowler's headquarters.

9. The Long Hike

It WAS now just before July 4, 1944, and I had decided to leave on July 5. This would give me a chance to go to the party that Lieutenant Johnston was giving on the night of the fourth. He had invited all of the girls for miles around. Plenty of tuba and homemade alcohol was to be available. His five-piece band was to play. Of course, Nanet was supposed to be there.

The party started at about 7:30 and finally broke up around three in the morning. We did a lot of dancing; we drank a lot of tuba and alcohol. Those present considered it a great party. We took the girls home and then went back to our own house. When I woke up the next morning. I had a terrible hangover. I figured I'd better put off the trip until the sixth. Albert (Johnston) had detailed a soldier, Private Bongalos, who was to go with me as my guide for the trip north to guerrilla headquarters. Bongalos was from Zamboanga City and had worked for the Johnston Lumber Company. He had been educated in the trade school there and was more educated than the average Filipino at Siokon. Also he spoke good English which made him especially valuable to me. We took it easy all day of the fifth, recovering from the party.

Before we left the morning of the sixth, I got together my meager possessions of a couple of pieces of clothing and my old Moro kriss that had been given to me. Albert gave me a single-shot, homemade 45-caliber pistol for my protection. All of my gear was packed in a homemade canvas knapsack which I carried. Bongalos was armed with only a barong. We left in the morning after some emotional goodbyes to Nanet and my other friends. I never saw Albert Johnston again, but I did receive several letters from him during the next year. He was most kind and generous to me. I owe him a debt of gratitude for his help that he extended during my stay at Siokon. Much, much later, in 1981, when I visited Zamboanga on a trip to the Philippines, I was saddened to learn that Albert Johnston had died some years after the war.

Before we left Siokon, we heard through the bamboo telegraph that Colonel McGee, who dived overboard at Zamboanga City, had indeed made his escape, worked his way into the hills, joined the guerrillas, and was now at a place called Vitali on the east coast of Zamboanga. This was good news.

79

I figured that I would see him later on after I got across the island to guerrilla headquarters.

Bongalos and I left early the morning of the sixth on our way to guerrilla headquarters in Misamis Occidental, roughly a 15- or 16-day hike away. We walked barefooted on what was a pleasant 15-kilometer walk to Baligian on the coast northwest of Siokon. The trails led first through the lowlands between the hills and in among the rice paddies, then through the cogon grass foothills, and finally up over several ridges.

At the top of the first ridge, Bongalos and I paused for a rest. We could look down into the valley and see Siokon and some of the houses that made up the settlement. We could see the house that we had just left a few hours before. I later learned through the bamboo telegraph and a letter from Lieutenant Johnston that the day after we departed, a Japanese float plane (a pontoon plane with a single pontoon in the middle and two small ones at the ends of the wings) drifted in and dropped a couple of bombs near the house we had left that morning. No one was injured, but it was interesting to note that even though we were more than 90 kilometers north of Zamboanga with no connecting road and only vinta or boat traffic or people walking on the trails, word had reached the Japs in Zamboanga that the American who escaped was at Siokon, so they sent the plane over to bomb the house!

Bongalos and I continued our walk on northward from Siokon. We passed several small barrios or individual houses occupied by Moros, and finally reached a little place called Point Saint Maria. Here we arrived in time for a dinner at a Moro datu's house. The house was built quite high, nine or ten feet above the ground, and it was really just a one-room bamboo/nipa shack. When we arrived and climbed up the notched pole, we were greeted by the datu, his wife, and a baby girl. The Moro datu insisted that we stay for dinner and overnight. We gladly accepted.

While we hiked that day, we encountered many leeches on the trail. We were glad to get out of the underbrush and the cogon grass and back onto walking along the coastline again. Leeches aren't particularly dangerous, but they are a nuisance. Many people say that a leech bite will always turn into a sore, but I never had one become infected. We used to scrape them off with a knife as soon as we discovered them. They were so numerous along the trail that you could see them on the leaves of the trees and on the blades of the cogon grass, waving their thin bodies in the air, trying to find a passing victim to latch onto.

The thing that did bother us on the walk were bajuca, or rattan thorns which would stick in our feet and then break off, leaving part inside. They would invariably become infected and cause an ulcer. In the tropics most small cuts or scratches will turn into an ulcer if not constantly tended to. For the lack of better medicine, we kept the scratches open with several applications of hot coconut oil every day. The scratches and leech bites then healed quickly.

We ate chicken and rice for dinner that night at the Moro datu's house. We also had Moro cakes made out of rice flour. Again I encountered the cake called *locot-locot,* and although it looked like a lump of coarse white steel wool, it tasted good when deep fried in coconut oil. We spent a pleasant night in the Moro's house. It was cool enough to pull up a thin cotton blanket. Of course, the mosquitoes were bad, but there wasn't much we could do about them except cover our heads with the cotton blanket.

Early the next morning, we borrowed a vinta from the datu and got two boatmen belonging to the volunteer guards. These guards were civilians, usually too old to be soldiers, who did odd jobs for the guerrilla organization. They did lookout duty along the coast, had boats for transportation from one point to another, and they acted as runners for the mail service. They did all of this without receiving any pay; without their services, the guerrilla organization would have had a much harder time being successful. Their service brought home to me how much the Filipino people hated the Japanese and to what ends they would go to help any organization that was fighting them. Later, in the campaigns of Misamis, Malabang, and Dipolog, I saw volunteer guards killed in action while delivering food to soldiers at the front line. They didn't receive any pay for their service at all.

More than 75 percent of the people on the island of Mindanao went to live in the hills when the Japanese came. If they did not join the guerrilla organization, they did everything they could to help the guerrillas. Of course, many of the people did stay in the towns with the Japanese, but they used to pass out information to our agents. Many of them had been rounded up and forced to live in the towns to support the Japanese troops that were garrisoned at various towns around the island.

The small vinta which the Moro furnished us was rather crowded with the four of us and our baggage, but it was much better than walking along the rocky beach. We traveled all the next day to Dikulum and all the next night and arrived the next morning at Panganuran, near the place where I had first come ashore. During the night, as we were sailing up the coast, a Jap launch passed us not more than 300 yards away, but for some reason they did not stop us. They probably assumed that we were just a native fishing boat as there were many along the coast. As the launch came toward us, I was asleep on the bamboo mat in the center of the vinta, but as they were passing, I happened to wake up. Seeing the Japanese launch so close, I was just on the verge of rolling over the side to swim ashore. If Bongalos had not stopped me, I would have. It's lucky that they did not challenge us because I don't think my one-shot .45 would have helped much. However, the launch passed and disappeared, and we continued on our way.

The next day was a pleasant sail up the coast. We came upon some Moro spear fishermen and we dropped anchor when I indicated that I wanted to dive with them. They were fishing in about 30 or 40 feet of water at the foot of a cliff. Under water the huge boulders broken from the cliff were encrusted with coral and sea gorgonians and fans. I borrowed a pair of goggles and a spear and slipped into the calm, crystal clear water. In the next hour or so we got six or eight fish that were from one to three feet in length. The fishermen assured us that the fish were all good to eat. We divided the catch; thanked them, and proceeded on our way. Many times I have recalled that enjoyable couple of hours.

At Panganuran, the little Moro village where I had previously spent the day, the Latin-speaking priest, when he saw me with an escort of volunteer guards and Bongalos and not in undershorts, was very friendly. I got an entirely different welcome now that he realized I was an American officer and commanded a bit of respect. He offered us another larger vinta, but we decided not to take any more chances, and I insisted that we walk the remaining kilometers to Lubason, the next guerrilla headquarters. We sent the two volunteer guards back with the boat to Baligian. We requisitioned some other volunteer guards from the Moro priest to carry our knapsacks and bags and started out the next morning after a breakfast of rice and our fresh fish, washed down with coconut milk.

I don't know what we would have done without coconut milk. Actually, it was not coconut "milk," but that's what everyone called it. It was really coconut water from the young coconuts which are green ones and called *butung* in the dialect. Whenever I was hiking in the hills, I would stop every hour or so and get Bongalos to climb a palm to get green coconuts. The water from any two coconuts never tasted the same, but was always cool and sweet. Sometimes the "milk" tasted like spring water and other times like it was flavored with vanilla. The taste always depended on the age of the nut.

We caught up with a mail runner on the trail. He insisted that we stay with him when we arrived in Lubason, so we continued on together. When we arrived late that afternoon it was raining steadily. Sometimes we walked on the soft sand of the beach and other times along the rocky beach. We trudged up trails which crossed high points of land that came right down to the sea. We were soaked to the skin by the rain when we arrived at the mail runner's house, but after a bowl of hot chicken soup and a change into my only other set of clothes, everything was okay.

Bongalos and I spread our mats or *banigs* – woven grass mats that you unroll and lay flat on the floor and sleep on – the way the real Filipinos sleep. I didn't wake until someone shook us the next morning. I had long since forgotten what a mattress felt like. For more than two years, I had slept on the floors in prison camp. The bamboo beds or floors with a grass mat which we were using now were actually comfortable.

One of the first things we had that morning was a drink made from tuba, chocolate, and eggs all beaten together in a glass. I had learned to like this drink, called a *cotta* when in Siokon. Later that morning we went to visit Lieutenant Casiño, the company commander in the guerrilla unit in Lubason. He insisted that we stay with him for a few days. I was getting used to Philippine hospitality and knew that it was useless to refuse. Besides, to have an American officer stay overnight gave him and his unit some prestige, so I felt obligated. My feet were sore from stone bruises as we had been walking good distances daily, sometimes up to thirty kilometers. Bongalos also wanted to visit a girl he knew in town, so that settled that.

While we were in Lubason, I met a Chinese family named Koo with two very beautiful daughters named Zutica and Nina. I went over to their house every afternoon for *merienda,* which is similar to the English custom of afternoon tea. They served cakes and coffee or chocolate. I talked to Nina and Zutica about Suliman University in Negros, where they had gone to school before the war. When the Japanese came, their family left Negros and came to this west coast of Zamboanga to be away from the Japanese. When Bongalos and I finally left, they insisted on giving me a going-away present of a shirt, pants and a towel, and above all, a can of Vienna sausage which they had been saving and which they dug up from their cache out in the yard. The one thing, however, that embarrassed me was their insistence that I take off my clothes to try on the shirt and pants so they could be sure of the fit. While I stripped down to my underwear, nobody felt compelled to leave the room.

Everyone stood there and watched while I tried on the new clothes. They had brought these things with them from Negros and had been saving them all along. They were certainly very generous to give me some of what they had been saving. I was beginning to realize that if you ever want anything and can't find it, all you have to do is go to a Chinese merchant in town, and he probably will have it or can locate it. It is another debt that I owe to my friends in the Philippines.

We had a big lechanado before I left. At that time I think I ate more roast pork than ever before or since. This group butchered the pig, stuffed it with rice, onions, chicken, and spices, and put it on a spit and barbecued it over a very slow fire, basting it with coconut oil. It took several hours to cook the pig through, and when finished, it was golden brown outside. The skin was real crisp and crunchy, the way barbecued pork skin is supposed to be. Mexicans and tropical people like it very much. The meat absorbs the flavor of the spices cooked inside. When you eat lechanado, you just break off pieces of skin and eat them and reach up and pull the tenderest kinds of meat you can find. The meat is real white and very good when hot off the fire. However, nothing is worse than cold lechanado the next day when the grease is solidified and cold. It is then just a blob of indigestion.

The next day we left Labason for Sindangan, however, we would not get to Sindangan that day. Our companions were a Mr. Yang and a Lieutenant Melicor. We walked 23 kilometers to Salug. We had hoped to catch a *kulumpit*, which is a kind of sail boat, for the balance of the trip to Sindangan, but it didn't arrive. We stayed overnight in the house of a Moro called Tongao. Twenty-three kilometers is a long walk barefooted over the sand and gravel beaches. Usually on nights after these long hikes, I sat on the edge of a stream and soaked my feet in the water because, even though toughened, they still throbbed and ached after that kind of hike.

The next day, we left for another walk along the coast in weather that was quite pleasant. I really enjoyed my freedom as I walked leisurely along the beaches of the Zamboanga coast. Except for my feet taking a beating on the trails, I really enjoyed life. I had plenty of food, I was among friends, and soon I would be striking back at the Japanese. I had made up my mind that I was not going out by submarine, but was going to stay on with the guerrillas.

That night we arrived in Bucanasi and stayed with a Chinese saltmaker. The next day we arrived late in the afternoon at Sindangan. Colonel Garma, commander of the 105th Division had his headquarters in Sindangan. We stayed with him overnight. My feet were holding out well, so I decided to leave the next morning. Colonel Garma had a small party that night for us. It was another enjoyable meal with tuba and the usual conversation. This time I didn't drink too much so we were able to leave the next morning. A nurse, Lt. Estella Remitio, wanted to go over to the headquarters at Misamis, and she had been waiting for someone who was going to cross the mountains. All agreed that she should go with us. Colonel Garma assigned a guard of five soldiers to go with us for the march across the mountain. Food was going to be scarce, he warned, so under the expert advice of Estella, we bought provisions for our trip. We carried one *ganta* (a large bag) of corn and rice mixed. We took 20 dried fish, a half kilo of sugar (about a pound), and several cups of salt. This ration was mainly for Lieutenant Remitio, Bongalos, and me. The soldiers were each carrying their own ration which consisted of a few handfuls of rice and some dried fish. We were able to pick up some avocadoes and fruit along the way.

When Colonel Garma told me that Estella was going with us, he said that she walked slowly and that would be convenient for me as I was barefooted. She had a pair of shoes. In the next two days, Estella took the lead and we averaged about 35 kilometers a day! So much for the "slow walker." Those were the longest hikes I have ever made in my life. Most of the walk was over gravel roads. For the next couple of nights, I did a lot of soaking in the streams when we arrived at our destinations. However, for my own protection after the first couple of days, I took over the lead and slowed the pace a bit!

On the last leg of the journey to a barrio called Punta, all of our feet gave out and we had to borrow a vinta for the last ten or fifteen kilometers into Punta. We embarked on the vinta at a place called Duhinob. The boat we acquired was a racing vinta of about 20 feet with a very large sail. We had the five soldiers, Bongalos, Estella, myself, and a couple of other hangers-on. When we loaded up, I knew the boat was overloaded, but as is typical, whenever there is a vessel going anywhere, there's always a bunch of people who want to go along. The badly overloaded boat was shoved off from the beach. About 700 yards off shore, the crew was putting up sail when a gust of wind caught us and we capsized. Everybody, of course, was thrown into the sea. Estella couldn't swim, but she hung onto the boat until help came. We finally got our boat back to shore and nobody drowned. I lost my pistol in the scramble and had to make the rest of the journey with only my kriss. We spent the rest of the morning on the beach with our clothes and possessions spread out on the sand to dry. We caught another boat that afternoon and arrived in Punta at dark. It was July 17, 1944. We stayed overnight with Captain Padayhag, the company commander of the guerrilla unit.

From Punta we were to leave the coast and cross the mountains to Misamis (a four-day hike), where I was supposed to meet Colonel Bowler, the commander of western Mindanao. At that time the guerrilla commander for the island of Mindanao, Col. W. W. Fertig, whom I later got to know very well, as I served on his staff, was still on the other side of the island in Agusan Province. Coming up from Siokon I had heard from a runner that Colonel McGee had gotten through and was on his way to A Corps also. He was traveling up the east coast of Zamboanga. I was certainly glad to hear this, as I hadn't given him much chance that night he went over the side off Zamboanga City.

On July 18 we started out on the trek across the Dapiak-Malindong mountain range. Our first stop was at a small barrio named Milad. We stayed with a Spaniard (a Basque) who had married a Filipina and had come to this remote place to escape the Japanese. He was a chess player and badly wanted to play. He used to play by mail with friends in Spain before the war. I was a lousy chess player, but couldn't refuse him. First we had supper. His wife fixed us a nice meal of coffee, rice and squash, and she had broiled two small mud fish from the rice paddies around the house. After the meal a bottle of Spanish brandy showed up, and we played chess until the wee hours. Of course he won every game, but I think he thoroughly enjoyed the time.

We made an early start the morning of July 19. We left the coastal plain, crossed some rolling hills, and began our hike into the mountains. We were to pass through previously unexplored territory. We would encounter no people other than widely scattered groups of Subano hill tribes who lived off the forest. As I looked up into those dark green heights, I felt like David Livingstone, the missionary and explorer in Africa. This was unexplored territory. This new trail had just been opened by the guerrillas between the west coast of Zamboanga and Misamis Occidental on the other side of the mountain range. I looked forward to this adventure!

Following the single-file trail, we entered the jungle, walked along stream beds, crossed innumerable canyons, and sometimes waded through the same river five or six times in a single morning.

The second night we stayed in an abandoned Subano village (Sibulan). One of the soldiers shot a monkey (the trees were full of them). He skinned the monkey, cut it up, and put it into a pot with rice, onions, and some corn with a bit of garlic for flavoring. The monkey meat wasn't too bad, and the men assured me that the piece I got was the best – a hand and lower arm. They all agreed that the flesh on the palm was the best! You couldn't prove it by me.

We were in the Malindong mountain range and at an altitude of about 7000 feet. It was cold at night and we huddled together on two banigs (mats) under a mosquito bar. Estella, Bongalos, and I were the only ones with thin cotton blankets. The men huddled around the fire which they kept burning all night.

The next morning a heavy mist obscured the view. We felt closed in by damp curtains as we chewed on some dried fish, ate fruit, and had hot coffee boiled in the one pot we had. We drank out of bamboo cups. The mist gradually burned off after the sun climbed above the mountain tops.

Some of the larger canyons took almost a day to cross and we used vines and tree roots to lower ourselves down the sides or to pull up the other side. The soldiers did a great job of carrying our bundles, their packs, and their rifles. The trees were a riot of birds and monkeys. Occasionally we saw a bunch of wild pigs. At night we could hear the mutjac, or barking deer in the forest.

The third night was a repeat of the night before, but this time we boiled up some dried fish and rice instead of monkey stew. We were at an even higher altitude and thus had to endure a much lower temperature. The fourth morning we trudged on and by noon we were moving down the other side of the mountain range. We arrived at the corps hospital at Parason late in the afternoon. I decided to stay overnight as it was still a three-hour hike to Colonel Bowler's headquarters. This was the night of July 21, 1944.

Estella was going to stay at the A Corps Hospital, which for safety was located about three days' hike from the town of Misamis, then occupied by the Japanese. Seven nurses, a dentist, and two doctors, Major Frias and Lieutenant Rivera, tended the sick or wounded. These nurses and doctors performed medical miracles with practically no equipment. At night they operated by flashlight! The buildings consisted of three bamboo and nipa

Top: Joe Coe relaxes on the front "steps" of the weather station at Dimorok in the hills of western Misamis Occidental Provence in August, 1944. *Bottom:* Luke Campeau, Max Hoke, Douglas, Ben Farrens, Watson and others with friends at the weather station at Dimorok.

palm structures located in the foothills and surrounded by coconut, banana, avocado, and cacao trees.

While I was at the hospital, I met the first American I had seen since my escape. Lt. Luke Campeau, who was from Montana, had come into the hospital for some dental work. He had arrived in Mindanao in May by submarine from Australia to set up an advance weather station in support of the coming invasion of the Philippines. His station was about four hours' hike from the hospital. He insisted on giving me a pair of canvas jungle boots (my first shoes since I had come ashore), a set of khaki clothing, cigarettes, and chewing gum (also all firsts). Luke eventually gave away so much of his own supplies that he didn't have any extra left for himself.

During the next two months while I was at A Corps headquarters and the radio station at Camp X, I would make the three or four-hour hike to the hospital every time I got a chance, not only for the good food served up by the dietician, Miss Buenafe, but to see Lt. Connie Avenceña, one of the nurses. We used to sit up at night by a coconut oil lamp and play rummy or she would teach me Visayan, the dialect in the southern islands. Connie was about five feet tall, with rich, wavy black hair, a nice figure, and a really great personality. She had been an army nurse for about six years with the Philippine Army before the war. Whenever I needed clothes mended, I would send them to Connie. Knowing my weakness for peanuts, she sent me some, roasted in coconut oil, every week by the mail runner.

With plenty of food available, and with good feminine companionship, prison camp was only a bad memory. I still wanted to settle scores with the Japanese, however, and hoped that the time when I could was not far away.

10. Guerrilla Headquarters

I FINALLY got away from the hospital at noon and arrived at A Corps headquarters late on July 22, 1944, 17 days after leaving Siokon. Colonel McGee arrived later that same night, soaking wet, after hiking since early morning. He was really surprised to see me, and we sat up late talking about what had happened since I had seen him last. Colonel Bowler was away at the time, so we relaxed at his house in the forest and let Zac, the Filipino cook, try to fatten us up.

Colonel Bowler's house was built from native lumber and located in the center of a large tract of forest. We had to lie low, staying in the forest, as the Japanese had just withdrawn their troops from a drive to try and capture A Corps headquarters and destroy the guerrilla movement in Misamis province. Using almost 1000 troops, they had come within three kilometers of where we were then living, and as they probably still had spies in the area, we didn't want to let them know we were living there.

During the next few rainy days I visited G-2 headquarters and debriefed them on the Jap troop ships and my escape. Colonel Bowler had received some records by submarine and since we had a phonograph, I heard "White Christmas" sung by Bing Crosby for the first time. I visited Colonel Cabili who was G-4 and he advised me that there were no uniforms or shoes available. Anyway, the ones given me by Campeau would last for some time.

Colonel McGee and I talked quite a bit. He had plans for a new guerrilla organization in Zamboanga. Once I went to the house of Lieutenant Lewis, a former Navy petty officer, who had come to Mindanao on the PT boats with General MacArthur from Corregidor, had been left behind, joined the guerrilla movement, and married a beautiful Filipina girl. His wife had invited me over for breakfast as she knew I still had not satisfied my craving for eggs after 26 months in prison camp without them. I sat down to a plate of six fried eggs, chorizos (native sausage colored with red achuete seeds), fried eggplant, rice, and coffee. When I had finished, Mrs. Lewis asked if I wanted any more. I had six more eggs scrambled with more chorizos and rice. It was the best breakfast I had during all of my time in the hills, one I will never forget.

Colonel Bowler arrived back at his headquarters the next day and for the next few days, we continued to rest up and discuss the organization of the guerrilla forces and what had been happening to them, and some of the plans for the future. Colonel Bowler got in touch with Colonel Fertig on the other side by radio and advised of Colonel McGee's and my arrival. In the next few days Colonel McGee decided to go to Australia by the first available submarine. I decided to stay in the Islands and even up a few scores I had to settle for friends I had lost in the 26th Cavalry and in prison camp.

I now learned the details of the guerrilla organization about which we had heard rumors while in prison at Davao. All of the guerrillas on Mindanao were organized into the Tenth Military District under the command of Col. W. W. Fertig, a former mining engineer from Suragao, who had been called to active duty when the war broke out. He had not surrendered and had stayed in the hills to organize the guerrillas. At first he had some trouble in organizing all of the separate bands into one command, but finally succeeded. He was one of the most capable leaders I have ever known, and in my estimation, accomplished an almost impossible job. When you consider that it took at least 24 days' hiking to get from Bowler's headquarters in Misamis Occidental to Fertig's headquarters in Agusan on the other side of the island, you can see what I mean. In spite of the distances to be covered, and the time it took to travel these distances, he organized the island into two corps. Each corps was divided into divisions. Each division was divided into regiments and so on down to squads. This was all accomplished during late 1942 and early 1943. Radio contact with MacArthur's forces in the Southwest Pacific was established in late 1942 or early 1943. The divisions were almost all commanded by Americans. Eighty-five Americans, officers and enlisted men, never surrendered to the Japanese and these were all serving with Colonel Fertig. Colonel Bowler commanded A Corps. Under him, he had the 105th Division commanded by Colonel Garma, the 106th Division commanded by Lt. Col. John McGee (not the McGee who went to Australia), the 109th Division commanded by Lt. Col. Grinstead, the 108th Division commanded by Lt. Col. Charlie Hedges. Colonel Hedges was also in charge of all Moro troops in Lanao.

I always liked to visit Colonel Hedges because he never failed to dig up an extra pack of cigarettes and make me feel at home. Capt. Don LeCouvre commanded the separate 121st Infantry Regiment which was stationed around Zambo City. He maintained outposts within one kilometer of the city where 8000 Jap regular troops were stationed. The 107th and 110th Divisions in Davao and Agusan were commanded by Lieutenant Colonel Childress and Lieutenant Colonel McClish. All of the junior American officers were either working at the different radio stations or serving or commanding regiments or companies in the different divisions.

Colonel Fertig, with help from Southwest Pacific Headquarters, had established coast watchers and air warning stations all around the island by early 1944. These stations reported to him the movements of Japanese sea and air traffic. These reports were sent immediately to MacArthur's headquarters in Australia.

Besides gathering intelligence information, the guerrillas in early 1943 had harassed the Japanese at every opportunity throughout the island of Mindanao. Colonel Fertig had approximately 35,000 men under arms at that time.

I had told Colonel Bowler that I wanted to lead some attacks on the Jap garrisons in Misamis province, but he advised that I would have to wait awhile as there were orders from MacArthur's headquarters for the guerrillas to lay low for the time being and confine their activities to intelligence gathering and reporting Jap naval and troop movements. (What we didn't know was that the landing in Leyte was being set up and the coast watchers and radio stations being sent in by submarine were in preparation for that action.)

For the time being, Colonel Bowler suggested that I go up in the mountains and help Captain Simmons set up a radio control station. Simmons had just brought up a lot of equipment by submarine and was to send reports directly to MacArthur's headquarters in Australia. Besides helping him, I was to consolidate reports on Jap air traffic received from our stations in different parts of the island and also send them to Australia. Simmons had located his camp in the unexplored Malindang range as positive security against the Japs. It was two days' hike from Colonel Bowler's house. In the next few days I got together the equipment Colonel Bowler had given me from his limited supply. I received first aid kits, toilet articles, a flashlight, ponchos, guns and ammunition consisting of a carbine and a Thompson submachine gun.

At the time I joined Colonel Bowler in Misamis, Colonel Fertig had his HQ in the Agusan River Valley in eastern Mindanao, almost 24 days' hike from Misamis. The Japs were still trying to exterminate him. He was pretty much on the run. Several times before, once in Lanao in the early days of the guerrilla movement in late 1942 and again in July, 1943, in Misamis Occidental, the Japanese had tried to wipe out the guerrilla movement. At that time at Davao Penal Colony the Japanese had announced that they had carried out a "punitive expedition against Colonel Fertig, the self-styled bandit leader, and with the help of the Imperial Navy and Air Corps, had succeeded in wiping out the bandits once and for all."

Since February, 1943, submarines had been landing supplies for the guerrillas and by mid–1944 we had hourly contact by radio with Southwest Pacific headquarters. Throughout the countryside by mid–1944 many telephone lines had been reestablished, using captured Jap wire and old dry cells soaked in vinegar and salt. Alcohol stills and coconut oil factories had been established. The alcohol, made from tuba and sugar cane, was used to

Letters sent and received by submarine from Mindanao. The letter to me has only the address "Mindanao" and it was delivered!

run old automobiles which were rehabilitated. The coconut oil ran diesel engines. Colonel Hedges repaired the lighting and the water systems in Iligan in mid-1944 so that the city was almost in its prewar condition.

In early 1943 only about 60 percent of the guerrilla troops had arms, by by mid-1944, everyone was armed. Submarines brought in 30 to 40 tons of supplies on each trip and in 1944, they made several trips a month.

In October, 1944, we opened the airfields at Misamis (Labo), Dipolog, and one which had been built with Subano labor in Central Zamboanga. This field was called "Farm #2." When these were completed, we began to receive supplies by C-47, C-46, and PBY planes. By the fall of 1944 the Japanese were pulling back from many of the towns in northern Mindanao and, except for a large force in Zamboanga City and a garrison in Misamis City and Malabang, the Japanese had pulled back from western Mindanao. The guerrilla forces had prepared themselves and the final struggle was soon to come.

11. Camp X

I DIDN'T want to go into the mountains and monitor air traffic. I wanted to strike back at the Japanese, but reluctantly I went up to Camp X, determined to get back down soon to see action against my former captors.

Bongalos and I, with two Volunteer Guard cargadores to carry our packs, left Colonel Bowler's house on August 16, 1944. We presented a different appearance from our former one when we were coming up from Siokon. We were now armed with pistols, a carbine, and a Thompson submachine gun. As we weren't in too big a hurry, we spent the night at the hospital with Connie and the others. We left early the next morning, and after an enjoyable walk through the foothills and into the forest, we stayed in Semata that night with Father Deigler. He was a Catholic priest who evacuated there when the Japanese came to Mindanao. He was formerly a teacher at the Atenao de Cagayan, but he was now devoting his time to converting the pagan Subanos. He had built a beautiful little plantation on the top of a hill and grew some of the best bananas and papayas I have ever eaten. He used to send them to Captain Simmons and me at Camp X. From his house on the hill you could see the surrounding country for miles. For some reason it reminded me of Blue Ridge Lodge outside of Waynesboro, Virginia, where I went to Fishburne Military School. From there I used to look down on the Shenandoah Valley.

From Semata the trail to Camp X went west into the mountains of central Zamboanga. All equipment and food for the radio station had to be carried over this trail by Subano cargadores. Each Subano would carry about 60 pounds! The Subanos averaged less than five feet in height and often their packs were bigger than they were. These carriers worked under a Mr. Gondamon, an educated Subano, who lived in Semata. Once in a while he would come up to the camp for a visit, and by acting as interpreter for me, he helped me collect a lot of data on the Subano customs.

It took five hours to get from Semata to Camp X. The newly cut trail wound through the forest, following the ridges, and now and then passed through a *caingin,* or clearing, where Subano families lived in their little houses built on poles. They would always hear us coming, and when we arrived, the clearing and the houses would be empty. Infrequently we caught a glimpse of someone in a clearing across a ravine. Later, after the trail had been used more, the Subanos got used to us and didn't run away anymore.

The trail crossed three deep canyons and forded the big Salug River which was so swift we had to hold hands and use poles to steady ourselves. For an hour we climbed straight up the other side of the canyon until we arrived at the small Subano settlement called Dampalan. The guides told us that Camp X was about 30 minutes walk away; but we sat down under one of the houses to rest. The climb didn't seem to have bothered the Subanos, but Bongalos and I were dripping with perspiration.

While we were resting, I decided to look in the house and climbed the notched log to the door. The house was ten feet off the ground. Inside there sat an old man who smiled when I came in. I sat down and offered him a cigarette, but as we couldn't talk to each other, we just grinned.

The house was one big room with the door and fireplace in one end and the slightly raised sleeping dais at the other. The house was 15 feet long and 10 feet wide. Except for a few clay pots, rattan fish traps, baskets, fish spears, a couple of knives, and other odds and ends, the house was empty. However, as in most Subano houses, there were several very old Chinese jars standing about. These were used to hold rice wine. The jars had been handed down from their ancestors and in a way were a measure of the wealth of that family. These jars were anywhere from 18 to 30 inches tall and about 14 or 15 inches in diameter, iron oxide color and decorated with dragons, lion heads, or other symbols. These jars had been moved to the Philippines in the period 1500 to 1600 from Fukien Province in China and originally were used to ship tea to the Philippines from China. Later, after the war, I asked Mr. Gondamon to get four of these jars for me. I still have them today.

In addition to the main house there was another smaller house nearby where the Subanos stored their rice and corn. The chickens and pigs were kept in cages under the house. Up in the rafters close to the roof in the main house, there was a little platform about four feet square. I later learned that this was for the young girls of the family. They slept there for protection. The girls climbed up, then pulled their little bamboo ladder up after them.

I was sitting in the house grinning at the old man when I heard an American's voice below on the trail. I knew the only person it could be was Simmons, so I let out a yell. At first he couldn't figure out who was calling him, or where the caller was located. I came out of the house and nearly broke my neck falling off the notched pole. Simmons, a big fellow from Ohio, at that time had a black goatee. I had never met Simmons so we introduced ourselves, had a cigarette, and went on up to the station.

Camp X consisted of four bamboo shacks in a clearing on top of a ridge between two mountains. We had a mess hall, a barracks for the Filipino boys, an engine shack, and a radio shack where the Americans lived. There were four other Americans, all lieutenants, working there with Simmons: Helliard, Bujonoski, Rutherford, and Douglas. They were all originally from the Air Corps and had been hiding in the hills since the surrender. They helped with the code work and maintenance of the radios.

Bongalos and I eventually got our camp built up using Subano labor with the help of Mr. Gondamon. We built a combination club house and mess hall and called it the "Yabo River Army and Navy Club" as it overlooked the deep Yabo River canyon. We constructed a bamboo shower on a little creek about 200 yards from our house. The only trouble was that we would get leeches all over us coming back from the shower.

Simmons had a lot of books he had brought with him from Australia and since it had been so long since I had read anything, I used to sit up late at night in the code room, reading by a diesel oil lamp. This was the first time I had seen the "pocketbooks" put out by the Army for the soldiers.

During those days Simmons worked harder, I believe, than anyone in the islands, and did a wonderful job in setting up the radio net control station. The radio sets required heavy diesel engines and other engines and equipment. Some of those parts weighed as much as 200 pounds. He got them all moved over the trail by Subano cargadores from A Corps and never once went off the air. The engines would break down and the radio sets went on the bum, but he always managed to keep operating. On top of that, he had malaria about every two weeks. We didn't have "sick leave" during guerrilla operations.

Bongalos built a three-room house for us to live in. It was 500 yards from the radio shack. He made bamboo bunks, tables, and chairs. The sides of the house were bamboo and the roof was made of cogon grass. The floor was typically Filipino, made of split bamboo, so we never had to worry about sweeping.

My work was such that I had a lot of time to myself, so Bongalos and I used to roam over all the trails, stopping at every Subano house we came to. I learned a lot of Subano customs and, by giving them empty cartridges, I made many friends. They sent me cucumbers, watermelons, eggs, and once in a while, a chicken. They also brought me from time to time something they called *pinipig*. It was made from glutenous upland rice. The Subanos pounded the kernels slightly, then toasted them over the fire until they swelled up and popped. It reminded me of puffed rice or rice crispies. The puffed kernels could be eaten dry or with a little brown sugar (which they produced in bowl-shaped discs) and some coconut milk. This was almost like having cereal at home.

The Subanos also took us deer and pig hunting. The deer were the size of a dog and very numerous. Simmons and I sat on my doorstep at night and listened to them "bark" in the forest down the hill. We tried hunting the deer at night, using a light, but I never got one. The natives would trap the deer and pigs in a trap that shot a sharpened bamboo spear across the trail when the animal stepped on a vine which acted as a trigger. They put these traps on the game trails and several times nearly speared some of us when we were roaming around. We finally got them to stop using the traps around our camp.

We went pig hunting several times, using Simmons' twelve-gauge shotgun. When the moon was full, we would wait for the pigs in the comote patches around the Subano houses. Whenever we got one, we would give part of it to the Subanos and take the rest back to camp. Some of the pigs had tusks over three inches long and could be nasty if they caught you on the ground. Just to be on the safe side, we shot them from bamboo platforms built in small trees.

While at Camp X I took the opportunity to make a study of the mountain Subano people who lived around us in widely separated groups. When we explored the country, Bongalos and I would start out early in the morning with a carbine, compass, medicine kit, and field glasses. The hills were criss-crossed with Subano trails, and we would take different paths every time we went out. We would spend the morning hiking away from camp, eat dinner in some Subano house, and come back to camp in the afternoon. We stopped at every house we came to for a few minutes to get the people used to seeing us. The houses were easy to locate as they were built on the hills and surrounded by a *caingin*, or cleared field. The Subanos believed that if they built their houses on the hill away from the rivers, the river spirits wouldn't get their children. Sometimes the houses would be a kilometer away from the water. They would keep a supply of water on hand in bamboo tubes. I am sure that building away from the streams kept many Subano tots from falling into the water and drowning.

When Bongalos and I came to a clearing on the trail, we pulled out our field glasses to pick out the house we wanted to visit. Lots of times we could get within a hundred yards of a house before being discovered. When someone did see us, all the women ran out of the house and disappeared into the brush or rice fields. That upland rice would usually be shoulder high and the family could disappear into it like quail. There wasn't any yelling or shouting, just a silent disappearing act. The men would sit quietly in the house when we climbed up the pole into the front door. Before entering we would give the conventional greeting, "Maayo," which meant "good morning" or "hello." When the men heard that, it put them at ease and they answered, "Daayon" which meant "come in." We didn't want to scare them and first impressions with them are important. After a few smiles and a cigarette around, things would start to loosen up.

The best way to make a Subano feel at ease is to show interest in what he is doing or the things he has made. I knew enough words to get along fairly well, even if Bongalos wasn't along; I made it a practice to always ask questions about everything.

The Subanos all chew betelnut. Once in a while I would mix up a chew in front of them to make the feeling more congenial. The chew is made of three ingredients: a piece of betel-pepper leaf, a small piece of betelnut from the areca palm, and a piece of lime made from burnt snail shells. All of this is chewed together and the result is a not unpleasant astringent taste. If you want it real strong, you add a piece of native tobacco leaf. The red color produced by the lime and nut will stain your teeth black, but this can be prevented by rubbing the teeth daily with the husk from the betelnut.

The Subanos have an interesting custom regarding the chewing of betelnut: if you are in love with a girl and want to let her know your feelings, you ask her to prepare a chew for you. If she consents, that means she will accept your attentions, or as the Filipino says, "She is negotiable."

The Subanos are a small people, averaging five feet in height, light brown in color, with straight black hair. Except for weaving baskets and mats and making abaca cloth, they have no other handicraft. Around their houses, they always have a couple of mangy dogs, a few chickens, and sometimes a pig or two. In their caingin they grow upland rice, squash, comotes, and cucumbers. They usually have a patch of native tobacco somewhere close by. In the mountains where the coconut tree does not grow and tuba is not available, the Subanos prepare a drink from rice called *pungasi*. To do this they take the cooked rice, mix it with water, and mash it into a ball about the size of your fist. Then they put these balls in the sun to dry hard. To make the wine, they put these balls in water in a closed clay jar and set it aside to ferment. They use this drink at weddings and other ceremonies.

Their weddings are very simple. The boy and girl decide to get married and they get the consent of their parents. The boy has to give the family of the girl a dowry, either money or the equivalent in chickens or rice. The amount varies according to the social status of the girl. Twenty pesos is the highest I have ever seen paid. After the dowry has been arranged, the family of the girl gets the head man of the community to perform the ceremony. Family members kill a chicken, and provide it for the head man who holds the girl's hand and the boy's hand in his own. The datu then murmurs wishes of good luck for them. He asks the spirits of the forest and rivers not to harm them. Then he paints both their palms with the blood of the chicken, using a certain kind of grass for the brush. After the ceremony, they have a feast and invite all of their friends. Later, after the couple has been married for a while, if the girl doesn't live up to the boy's expectations, he can send her back home and demand his dowry. Whether he gets this back must be decided by the datu or head man. The term "datu" is more or less a synonym for "chief."

On the trails through the forest while visiting the Subanos, Bongalos and I would run into wild pigs and deer, especially early in the morning and late in the afternoon. The trees were full of calao, or hornbills, large woodpeckers similar to our pileated woodpeckers, and other small birds. There were hundreds of monkeys and many times we surprised a group of them, bathing and playing in the water like children. They would run and hide when they saw us, but if we remained still for five minutes, their curiosity got the better of them, and they would start to chatter, come out of hiding, scream and make faces at us. Several times we saw pythons in the trees or a cobra gliding across the trail. The Philippine cobra is beautifully marked in black and bright yellow. The natives were always glad to get the skins of these to make belts or covers for their knives.

On one of my roaming trips, I was about half a mile from camp, walking along a trail through a bamboo grove when I saw a black tail disappearing into the underbrush. I stepped on the tail, then began to pull the snake out a little at a time. When I finally got it out, it was a beautiful specimen of a cobra about six feet long. Holding it by the tail and back of the head, I took it back to camp so all could see it. I was careful not to be bitten. In spite of the small fangs, the poison is deadly. We later killed the snake and gave the skin to the Subano datu who was quite pleased. From then on I was known as the "buang Americano." "Buang" means "crazy."

I never tired of roaming around the mountains and planned some day to go back and make a pictorial record of the Subanos and their country. There are still some burial caves that I have not seen. Mr. Gondamon promised to take me to visit them. As a kid in Virginia I was always fascinated with the life of the Indians, the wilderness, and travel in remote areas. Books about the Indians by the author James Willard Schultz were my favorites. When I stood there in Zamboanga on a trail three or four hours from camp and looked across a deep valley and saw only unending forest on all the mountainsides in sight, I somehow felt that I was experiencing the tales I had read about. I will never forget the exhilaration of those trips in that unexplored country.

Our normal diet at Camp X consisted of rice, mongo beans, a bean something like a blackeyed pea, chickens, and sometimes beef or pork brought up from Semata. Several times when the weather was bad and the carriers couldn't get over the trail, we had to eat monkey meat and corn, which we got from the Subanos by trading them some of our spare clothes. We had a small garden in front of the radio shack and grew beans, onions, garlic, and pepper.

Once we received a shipment of pig meat sent up to us, carried on a pole by two Subanos. We laid the meat out on the table and could already taste the feast we were going to have: roast pork. We unwrapped the banana leaf covering and began to prepare the meat but we noticed an odd texture. On closer examination we saw that this pork was completely infested with trichinosis larvae. The meat was full of little cysts. We dared not eat it even though we had been without any good meat for days. We buried it in the jungle so none of the Subanos would eat it. We went back to corn and monkey meat.

I was able to get one of the Subanos, a girl, to do my laundry by giving her some soap and some thread once in a while. Her name was Ukpi and she was in her early teens. Over the period of the next month and a half, I got to know the Subanos very well. They were used to my wandering into their houses at any time. With my medicine kit I treated many cuts and infections, gave out quinine, and did other first aid treatments. I remember one young girl about 15 or 16 that I ran into at one of the more remote huts in the forest. She had a terrible yaw or ulcer on her left cheek and had it covered with a piece of abaca cloth. I insisted on looking at it and she finally let me. The ulcer was about as big as a fifty cent piece and about one-fourth inch deep. I cleaned it up with bichloride of mercury and covered it with sulfa powder. I left a supply of bichloride of mercury and sulfa with instructions on how to use them. She and her parents seemed so grateful and thanked me profusely as I left. I hope they kept up the treatment as she was such a pretty girl. I never saw them again.

Whenever I got a chance and could spare him, I sent Bongalos down to the hospital and had Connie buy some eggs at the market there. Whenever he went down, she never failed to send back some roasted peanuts. Several times I went down for an overnight visit and stopped at our alternate radio station to see Campeau on the way back. He and Lt. Max Hoke ran the weather station. They sent out reports by radio direct to Australia.

The longer I stayed at Camp X the more I liked it. We were surrounded by mountains on all sides, and from my front porch, I could look across the Salug River Valley at Mt. Malindang, towering 8000 feet into the clouds. In one of the gorges on the mountainside, I could see a waterfall half buried in the green jungle. Simmons and I always planned to go over and look at it, but we never got the chance. It was about two days' hike away. Our camp was at 7000 feet above sea level and the nights were so cold we had to wrap up in our blankets and ponchos. Coconut oil would solidify at night so the temperature had to be about 50 degrees Fahrenheit. The sun was usually out for three hours in the morning at that time of the year and the rest of the day was cloudy. It often rained in the late afternoon. In the mornings the mist lay in the canyons and ravines until the sun came out about nine or ten o'clock. After the hot, dry days in the lowlands, this kind of weather was a welcome change.

It is interesting to note that by the time I left the Subano country, I was pretty well accepted. This was proved by the fact that a few days before I was to leave for good, I was sitting in the datu's house, passing the time when out of the clear blue sky Ukpi came over, sat down in front of us, took out the betel box, and proceeded to mix a chew which she then offered me. I was somewhat taken back, knowing what it could mean. The datu looked at me with a smile on his face, so I had to accept the offer and proceeded to chew along with him. Ukpi shyly withdrew and in a little while, I had to leave. Luckily I left a few days later and didn't have to fulfill the implied contract!

We got word from our radio station in Sindangan one day in late September that a Jap transport carrying American prisoners had been torpedoed a few miles off shore. About 83 Americans survived and our station sent us a list of the names. Among them I recognized the names of many men I had known in Davao. These men were originally from our prison camp there, but had been out on a work detail when we moved. The men had completed the airfield that they were building at Lasang in Davao Province and were being moved north to Japan. The ship was not marked as carrying American prisoners and had been partially loaded with Japanese troops. An American submarine torpedoed the ship without knowing that there were Americans on board. The Japanese had machine gunned a lot of the men in the water, and out of the 750 on board, only 83 had managed to get to shore and were picked up by units of the 105th Division under Colonel Garma. Most of them were wounded and were cared for and clothed by Filipino families.

As soon as I heard about this, I wired Colonel Bowler and asked him to let me go over to that area to see what I could do to help. He replied that I had better stay at Camp X and make my reports. That was the one time I almost disobeyed orders. I had been in prison with those men for two years and wanted to see and talk to them and find out what I could do to help them. Several of my very good friends were lost on that ship, including the officer with whom I used to live in Manila. Colonel Bowler sent over a lot of medicine for them and arranged to have them picked up by submarine and taken to Australia. Colonel McGee went out with them. One of the survivors, Sergeant Coe (later made lieutenant), stayed with us to help with the radios. He had been a radioman with the 19th Bombardment Squadron during the war and volunteered to stay and help us. I saw him later and got the story of the sinking.

It seems that after Colonel McGee and then I had escaped, the Japanese weren't taking any chances. The men in subsequent POW transports were kept under closed hatches and all food and water was passed down to them by buckets. They were locked in the hold when the torpedo struck their end of the ship and ripped off the side. Coe said he had to climb over dead bodies to get out.

12. Attack on Misamis

ON OCTOBER 10, I got orders from Colonel Bowler to turn over my reports to Captain Simmons and come down to A Corps headquarters. Although I liked the life at Camp X very much, I had been asking Colonel Bowler if there wasn't something I could do where there was some action against the Japanese. I still had lots of debts to pay.

Bongalos and I got everything together, turned over our house to lieutenants Douglas and Helliard, told Simmons goodbye, and started down the hill. When we passed the datu's house, I didn't see Ukpi anywhere in sight. We hurried along the trail and spent the first night at Semata. Father Daigler was away at the time, so we stayed with Mr. Gondamon and his family. We had a nice meal and after a few glasses of tuba, turned in. Mr. Gondamon had several children, one of whom was a girl named Vicenta, about 16 or 18 years old. Like her father, she was large for a Filipino but a very nice looking girl. Her skin was a light golden brown and her black hair fell to her waist. She had a beautifully proportioned, fully developed figure. She sat around while we talked but didn't have much to say.

I was sleeping on the floor on a banig in a room by myself. We got up early the next morning to be on our way. I had just finished dressing when Vicenta came in, threw her arms around my neck, backed me up against the nipa wall, and gave me a long, hard kiss on the mouth! In the next moment she was gone. I stood there stunned for a few moments. I finished dressing, we ate breakfast, and left. I didn't see Vicenta anywhere. She had run out into the banana grove. Maybe I should have followed her but again, I decided it wasn't the time to get involved. I was not to see Vicenta again until two months later in Misamis City.

We passed the hospital and arrived at Colonel Bowler's house by early afternoon. Lieutenant Sinclair and Major Gillon had just arrived and were staying there also. Gillon had just come from Zamboanga and was on his way to Lanao and left the next day. He was going over to work for Colonel Hedges and Major Blow, another Australian. They were inspecting all Moro troops in Lanao, trying to get an accurate account of the number of men and arms. Lieutenant Sinclair had just come up from Australia by submarine and didn't have any assignment yet; so we both sat around the house for a few days. We spent this time roaming around the country.

On Sundays we would go down to the barrio Parasan about two kilometers away and watch the carabao fights. These were held in a big arena built of logs. Two bulls were put inside and the audience would bet on the fight. We just had fun watching. The defeated bull would quit fighting and run away, although the fight did get rather bloody. Colonel Bowler had a battery radio and we would listen to the news every night. Lieutenant Lewis, another American working with the quartermaster, had rigged up an automobile generator to a water wheel and kept the batteries charged that way. One evening, October 19, we were listening to the radio while sitting on Bowler's porch and heard them announce the landing on Leyte. We had been expecting the landing but didn't know what island it was going to be on. We never even thought of Leyte. For days before the landing there had been lots of P-38's and Liberators in the air over Mindanao. All the important targets on the island had been bombed heavily. The town of Cagayan, Cotabato, Davao, and Zamboanga had been reduced to ashes. We saw many dog fights and our troops recovered some of our pilots when their planes crashed in our territory. We would call in a Catalina plane to pick them up.

Colonel Bowler had been waiting for some special orders from MacArthur's headquarters. On October 19, 1944, the orders came in. We were to openly attack all Japanese garrisons where possible. The Japs were trying to rush troops from Mindanao to Leyte, and by attacking, we could tie a lot of them down. Colonel Bowler decided to send me down to direct the attack against Misamis, to be carried out by the 106th Infantry Regiment under Major Bonilla, a former school teacher from Jolo. Sinclair had left two days earlier to set up a new coast-watcher station in the hills back of Misamis town, and I was eventually to join him there at barrio Karangan, three days' hike away. Bongalos, my striker, and I again packed up and on two borrowed native ponies, left Colonel Bowler's headquarters on October 21. I was anxious to get back into the fight against the Japanese, and looked forward to the attack on their garrison at Misamis.

I had not been on a horse since before the surrender, and I certainly felt good not to be walking. The horses were only 10 or 11 hands high, and when I was in the saddle my feet almost touched the ground. In spite of their size, those little horses can carry a man 30 or 35 kilometers a day for days on end. Our big American horses in the 26th Cavalry were not supposed to travel more than 25 kilometers a day. Our saddles were carved out of a piece of wood and had been modeled after the old army McClellan saddle. Most of them were just plain wood but some were covered with leather. The one I had was plain wood and it got pretty hard after the first ten kilometers; but it was still better than walking. It made me feel like a cavalryman again.

I was to meet Major Bonilla at his headquarters in Dimalco about 25 kilometers away and make plans with him for the attack on Misamis City. In the meantime I learned that I had been promoted to captain as of October 22, 1944. In addition I had finally gotten my long awaited wish: I was off to even up a few scores with the Japanese.

At this time the Japanese had isolated garrisons at a number of towns in western Mindanao. In Zamboanga City they had several thousand troops, in Pagadian and Malangas about 200 troops, in Cotabato at Malabang about 700 troops. In the province of Misamis Occidental about 110 troops were stationed in Misamis City. The garrisons at Oroquieta and Jimenez had been pulled back to Cagayan. The garrisons in Lanao at Iligan, Momungan, and Liangan were in the process of being pulled back. The main strength of Japanese troops in Mindanao at that time was at Zamboanga City, Cotabato City, Davao, Cagayan, and on the north-south road between Cagayan in the north and Davao and Cotabato City in the south. There were also some troops in Surigao and Bukidnon in eastern Mindanao. By eliminating the Jap garrison at Misamis City, the province of Misamis Occidental would be free of Japanese.

Colonel Fertig also wanted to open the airfield at Labo about six kilometers outside Misamis City so that we could begin receiving supplies by air from MacArthur's forces in Leyte.

Bongalos and I took our time, traveling mostly at a walk, only trotting once in a while to break the monotony. It was hot and dry and the trees in the distance simmered in the bright sun. There wasn't a breeze stirring. We were on a carabao trail in open, rolling country. There was no shade. The open fields, planted in corn, stretched in front of us and back to the foot of the mountains that we had recently left.

We stopped at noon at a small barrio to get something to eat and drink and to wait for the cargadores who were carrying our luggage. As an American was still a curiosity, we ate our dinner of fried eggs, pork and rice with about 30 friendly Filipinos in a circle around us watching. We still didn't have any knives or forks, so I proceeded to eat Filipino style with the first two fingers and thumb of my right hand. I had been doing it so long I could eat with the best of them.

We rested about two hours, drinking a few glasses of tuba as it was too hot to travel during the noon hour. The little *tienda* (store) where we had stopped was just a bamboo framework with a nipa palm roof and a split bamboo counter. We sat on a bamboo bench. Behind the counter a couple of demijohns of tuba proved that this was really a beer joint with a small wood stove where the owners could cook. The most interesting thing, however, was the enticement offered to beer drinkers. The cost of a beer (tuba) was about 200 centavos. The patron took the fly-encrusted piece of abaca fiber off the top of a demijohn, poured out the foaming glass of tuba into a much-used glass which he had rinsed off in a pan of used water, and then handed you a section of smoked octopus (pulpo) arm from which the customer was free to cut or bite off a piece. The same tradition offered in US beer joints provided a hard-boiled egg or a pickle. The tuba was slightly reddish, as mangrove bark had been added to it to keep it from turning to vinegar too quickly. The octopus meat was reddish black from smoking, somewhat tough, but better than nothing. This particular octopus arm came from a large octopus and was two to two and a half inches in diameter with the suction cups still on!

Everyone gathered around wanted to know where we were going, but we gave them the usual vague, typically Filipino answer: "There-o" with a wave of the hand toward the horizon which seemed to satisfy their curiosity. They offered us fried bananas, cakes, and fruit. In all of my trips the people we met were so glad to see an American and would express their faith in MacArthur's return. Many times they would force me to take a bottle of beer or a can of sardines that they were saving to celebrate MacArthur's return. It was simply impossible to refuse the gift.

We arrived at Dimalco at about 4:30 p.m. and met Major Bonilla and his officers. Major Bonilla was a big man for a Filipino, about five feet, eight inches, and weighing about 170 pounds. He was very active and a good officer. Over the next few months I got to know him very well, and after two campaigns, I still ranked him as one of the best Filipino officers in the guerrilla movement.

After greetings were over, Bongalos and I went to the creek for a bath with the usual audience. Rural Filipinos usually bathe at public wells or in a creek and wear underwear shorts or slips as the case may be. I still felt a little funny, bathing in underwear shorts, but that's the only way when you have a mixed crowd of onlookers!

Bonilla and I made our plans that night and he sent runners to all his units, alerting them for the move to the first assembly points. His companies were scattered all up and down the province of Misamis Occidental and in these messages the troops were given certain destinations at which to assemble around the town. They were also to send one officer to the place Bonilla and I would be to receive further orders.

At this time Bonilla had about 400 men in his regiment; however, only 200 of them were armed—with Enfield rifles, Thompson submachine guns, Browning automatic rifles, and three 81mm mortars with 150 shells. Any resupply of ammunition and supplies had to come from A Corps headquarters and Colonel Cabili's S-4 supplies, two days' hike away.

The Japanese in Misamis City had fortified the town with pill boxes and block houses around the edges of the town. Their headquarters was in a large house in the center of town. They stored their supplies in the old Spanish Cota (fort) down on the beach by the pier. At that time the Japs still

Top: The old Spanish fort (the Cota) at Misamis served as headquarters for the Japanese at the time of our attack on October 31, 1944. (These two photos taken in 1947.) The 30-foot high walls which were also 20 feet thick, provided excellent protection for the enemy. *Bottom:* The main entrance to the Cota, now occupied by a Philippine Army Unit.

had radio contact with their other garrisons and by seaplane which called about twice a week. Some coastal boats made regular contact also.

The Japs were armed with rifles, automatic rifles, knee mortars, grenades, and a .30-caliber, water-cooled machine gun. About 200 Filipino citizens were forced to live in the town with the Japanese. All of these Filipinos were members of the Japanese enforced "Neighborhood Society," an organization to unite the Filipinos under the "new order." Our strategy was to attack the town from three sides, drive the Japs back into the Cota, then call in an air strike to bomb them out.

The country around Misamis City was flat, cultivated in rice fields and coconut groves. Just to the south of town, about two kilometers away, was a tall, isolated knoll called Bucagan Hill, about 500 feet high. On top of this hill were the remains of an old stone Spanish lookout. The Japs rotated a garrison of 20 or 25 men on the hill. In our plan we were going to attack Bucagan Hill as a primary objective, take it, and set up an 81mm mortar to shell the town and the fort. From Dimalco the regimental headquarters moved out to Kenuman Norte near Simmons' coast-watcher station. We were now 12 kilometers from the town of Misamis. While we were in Kenuman Norte, our lookouts one day spotted a coastal boat approaching Misamis City, and we suspected that the Japanese were going to reinforce the town or evacuate it. We had troops stationed along the coast and were prepared to repel the boat if necessary. However, the boat did not stop at Misamis and proceeded east in Iligan Bay and disappeared in the distance.

The next few days we spent getting the troops moved into their prearranged bivoac areas around the town. We moved our advanced headquarters down to Karangan, about four kilometers out of town.

I'll never forget the thrill and pride which ran through me when I saw those long lines of barefoot guerrillas winding up and down the rolling hills toward Misamis town. Some were carrying bundles of equipment and others carried mortar ammunition and boxes of rifle ammo slung on poles. In front of them were the fighting men armed with rifles and wearing bandoleers of bullets across their chests. Some wore shorts and shirts made of abaca fiber, others wore faded dungarees or khaki. Most wore straw hats of some kind. A few had helmets. All of them were happy; this was what they had been waiting for, no more ambushing and running. Now they were going to launch an all-out attack. They were confident they could win. Most of the men were volunteers in the guerrilla and had never had much real training except in how to shoot the weapons they carried. They were on their way to attack a garrison of seasoned Japanese in a fortified town. They were eager to get on with it. Every barrio we passed through turned out in force to wish us well. They rejoiced to see us because they knew that liberation was not far off. They already knew of the American landings in Leyte which had begun on October 19.

At our advanced headquarters in Karangan, Sinclair had set up his radio and had daily contact with Colonel Bowler's headquarters at Dimorok. We set up our supply base and spent the next several days reconnoitering the country and making sure the units were in their positions. Bonilla had the Volunteer Guards organized to carry supplies to the front and to evacuate any wounded to the hospital two days' hike away.

The regimental S-4 had a sufficient supply of rice on hand for the companies on the line. For meat and vegetables the companies sent out their own procuring details. This was necessary because of transportation difficulties and the fact that it was much harder to buy those things in large quantities. First-aid men were assigned to every company, and we had a dressing station in the regimental area. The only means of communication in the regiment was by runner. Later on during the siege, we were to activate the telephone lines to the other barrios.

By October 30 everything was ready and we launched our attack on the town from the north, west, and south at dawn on October 31. Our mortars had been moved up at night and the attack opened when we shelled the Japanese outposts. We then sent in the troops. There were swamps and rice paddies surrounding the city and there were only three points of attack possible. Consequently, on entering the city, our troops ran into stiff resistance from the Japanese strong points and the advance bogged down. We continued to shell the strong points and during the day number three and number four were knocked out with direct mortar hits on the houses the Japs occupied.

The assault on Bucagan Hill had failed under heavy Japanese fire and Sinclair, Bonilla, and I went over to see what we could do. By this time it was late in the day and we returned to our command post. After sending out runners to all units to hold and push during the night, I decided to move a mortar over to Bucagan Hill and shell it at dawn with about ten rounds, then attack the hill.

At dawn the mortar crew set up about 900 yards from the hill. We sent some scouts to probe the hill and they came under auto-rifle fire. The hill was covered with brush and coconut trees, but with glasses we could see the Japs once in a while. We called in the lieutenant commanding the troops around the base of the very steep hill and ordered him to attack after the tenth shell had been fired. I decided to go with the attacking troops to give them encouragement. I was armed with a Thompson submachine gun and several grenades and my .45-caliber pistol.

The mortars fired at about three-minute intervals. With glasses we could see two direct hits on the crest and Japs running between the trees. We moved up the hill, at times having to climb hand over hand, and laying down a covering fire. When we reached the top, we found that the Japs had pulled out; luckily, as we were all done in from the climb and would have put up a poor fight, I'm afraid. We found evidence of casualties, but they had taken their wounded with them. Their camp was a wreck, and there were two direct hits on their kitchen area. We recovered some raincoats, gas masks, grenades, and cooking utensils. Two of our men were wounded in the assault.

From the top of the hill we could see every house in town and the Cota. The crew moved the 81mm mortar up and were ready to fire in less than an hour after we had reached the top. The Jap troops had escaped back to town through the swamp and across the river. By runner we learned that the Japanese were holding out at the Misamis Institute on the west of town. If we could knock it out, we could enter the town at that point and flank their other positions. The mortar crew got two direct hits on the institute, then dropped the last four shells into the Cota on an extreme range of about 2300 yards.

When we got back to the command post, we learned the Japs had pulled out of the Institute with casualties and that we had advance patrols into the edge of town. There was some firing during the night, and at dawn we went to the Institute and learned that the Japs had pulled back into the Cota. However, there were a few snipers still in town and our patrols were trying to locate them. The roof of the Institute building had been hit by a mortar shell and there was a lot of blood on the floor. The Japs had, however, taken their casualties with them. Outside in a pill box covered with palm fronds, I found a knee mortar and two boxes of shells. The Japs left so fast they had to leave these behind. Later I would put that mortar to good use against the Japs in the Cota.

We went into town on November 1 and met the first bunch of civilian evacuees coming out. They were carrying everything they could. Most were old men or women or young children. They begged us not to kill them. I guess the Japanese had told them that the "bandits" would kill them if they were captured. They were terribly undernourished and some of them looked so pitiful that tears came to my eyes. We sent them back to collection areas under guard until we could weed out the actual collaborators. Some of these people had helped guide the Japs on their patrols and had been responsible for the deaths of many Filipinos living outside of town.

We walked on into town and headed for the cathedral so we could get up in the tower for a good view of the Cota. As we were foolishly walking down the main street, a sniper fired from one of the houses about a block down the street. I think we were in the ditch before the bullet ricocheted off the street where we had been standing! From the sharp crack of the rifle, I knew the Japs were firing the 6.5 round. Two more shots were fired and one bullet hit a soldier in the thigh. Luckily, it didn't hit a bone, and he was sent back to the hospital.

The patrols cleared out the town that morning, and we moved up our

The guerrilla hospital used during the attack on Misamis City was set up in a former Philippine government building about two kilometers out of town.

troops and set up our mortars in the church yard to shell the Cota. The range was about 600 yards. We set up an observation post in the town's empty cement water tank.

The town of Misamis had a population of about 2000 before the war. The water and electrical systems were destroyed when the Japanese took over and had never been repaired. The town was grown up in weeds and many of the houses were wrecked. As usual the Japanese had fixed up a few houses for their use but let the rest go. With all their promises to the Filipino people about the "Co-Prosperity Sphere," they had made no attempt to help rebuild any of the damaged property. As a matter of fact, they usually pulled out any plumbing, wiring, pipes, or machinery and shipped it off to Japan. I noticed that was true all over the Philippines.

During the late afternoon we continued to move our troops into town and established a line on the edge of the open ground surrounding the Cota. Our line was established around the three sides of the Cota. The other side was on the beach. The line was located in the houses nearest the Cota, and our troops dug in and started digging permanent trenches under the houses during the night.

In the late afternoon we sent in one of the civilians with a white flag to the Japanese with a demand for surrender signed by Major Bonilla, Sinclair, and myself. As I suspected, the Japanese commander sent back one word:

"Dami" meaning "no good." The civilian told us that the Japanese would not surrender to us "bandits" because they were sure we would kill them. We wouldn't have killed them if they had surrendered, but we sure intended to do so now!

That night I sent word by radio through A Corps to Colonel Fertig at Tenth Military District that the Japs were in the Cota, and I gave an exact description of how the planes could locate the Cota and how they should make their runs in from the land side toward the water to avoid any overages from hitting our troops. The next morning we got word that it would be awhile before headquarters could send planes as they were all fully occupied at Leyte and that we should keep the Japs under siege.

Our total casualties for the assault on Misamis were 9 killed and 15 or 20 wounded. It was during this campaign that Major Frias, Dr. Rivera, Dr. Incarnación and Dr. Garrella did such fine work in treating the wounded. With a few boxes of plasma and sulfanilamide, they and the nurses worked wonders. Connie was still working in the hospital and kept me informed on the good work they were doing there.

Another group organized by a Mrs. Capistrano and called the Women's Auxiliary Service helped a great deal toward the success of the guerrilla movement in Mindanao. Their work, together with the Volunteer Guards, brought home to me the importance of having the people behind a guerrilla operation. Without the help of the people of the country, a guerrilla organization is doomed to failure. The Women's Auxiliary delivered food and cakes to the soldiers, canvassed the barrios for clothes and blankets, and worked in the hospital tending wards, making bandages, and even contributing medicine. Both of these organizations received no compensation other than the satisfaction that they helped to defeat the Japanese. Without Mrs. Capistrano and the W.A.S. girls, things would have been pretty dull during the months of the siege. We used to look forward to the Wednesdays and Fridays when a group of girls would come to our headquarters with cakes and candy. Some of those girls walked 12 kilometers to make that trip to town from their houses in the *bukids* (mountains).

After our lines were established around the Cota, we began to move the rear elements into town. The battalion command posts and their aid stations moved up and occupied houses in town. Company command posts were right on the front line. Regimental headquarters was moved into the big house the Japanese had occupied as it was in good condition. Sinclair and I moved into a house near the cathedral which was in the center of town.

Once the Japanese were confined, we pulled several companies out of the line and stationed them on beach patrol north of Misamis town. There was still a chance that the Japanese at Cagayan might send over reinforcements by launch, and we wanted to be sure about it before they were

UNITED STATES FORCES IN THE PHILIPPINES
Field Headquarters

TO: Japanese Commander, Misamis Garrison

1. Your garrison is completely surrounded by our forces.

   Your situation is hopeless.

2. To eliminate needless sacrifice on your part, we

   demand your surrender.

3. You may come out with your staff officers displaying

   a large white flag following the national highway

   Tangubward where you will be met by our representative.

4. We guarantee your safety during and after this

   negotiation in accordance with the articles of

   land warfare.

M.S. BONILLA
Major, USFIP

DONALD H. WILLS
Capt. Cav. AUS

T.L. SINCLAIR
Lt. (sg) USN

DHW/mdn

Typed on tablet paper, this demand for surrender was sent to the Japanese Cota
commander carried by a white-flag–bearing Filipino. The Japanese commander
replied "Dami" ("no good") and the siege continued.

knocking at our back door. Our only communication with the towns to the north, Jimenez and Oroquieta, was by runners. If the Japs landed at Oroquieta about 40 kilometers up the coast, they could be down to us just as quick as a runner.

This eventually did occur. Several weeks later, when about 200 Jap troops landed at Oroquieta from two launches, we heard about the landing and were planning how to handle it when, luckily, the Japanese, after staying overnight, decided not to march on Misamis, got back into their launches the next morning, and went back to Cagayan.

I was sweating that one out and slept with my Thompson that night as I was apprehensive that our troops could not stop a force of 200 Japanese. We didn't even have that many fighting men and besides, we were low on ammunition and temporarily out of 81mm mortar shells, waiting for a supply from A Corps G-4, Colonel Cabili.

On several other occasions during the month of November, Japanese launches passed the Cota and tried to signal the men inside but withdrew hastily when we fired at them with the 81mm mortar. They returned to Cagayan on the other side of Iligan Bay.

The siege dragged on with sniping back and forth between the lines. We still shelled the Cota with our 81mm mortars but shells were in short supply. We had the range perfect at 825 yards and fired only at night just to keep them awake. We were carrying out a war of nerves. We also had the little Japanese knee mortar I had found at the Misamis Institute. I got a big kick out of shooting their own shells back at them. I fired from a position about 300 yards from the Cota. I took the fuse out of one of the shells and shot it into the Cota to be sure they knew it was their own ammo.

Things were pretty dull during the siege and we thought up many ways to make things more interesting. We would go down to the lines before breakfast and with field glasses and a rifle, we would look for a likely target. At the distance between the lines and the Cota of only about 250 yards, we could see the whites of their eyes. We would take turns firing with the other man watching. We called it the "morning turkey shoot." The only trouble was in firing from one place too long. The Jap snipers would pick out your position from the muzzle blast and things could get pretty hot as the Japs were doing the same thing we were. They were mostly using the high velocity 6.5 caliber rifle and the bullets hitting the sand continually showered us with sand. On one occasion I stayed in a spot too long, a sniper located me, and a 6.5 round missed my head by about two inches. I heard it whip by, and it sprayed me with concrete fragments. I picked up the round and found it still hot. I later had it engraved with the date and I still have it today. I figure that was the bullet with my name on it. I'm thankful it missed. We soon learned to move position after firing two or three shots. Then we would sit back and laugh at them for shooting at the old spot.

Here I am with some "friends" during the siege of the Cota during October and November, 1944.

On another occasion early in the siege, one of the Jap soldiers must have thought he had a charmed life or that the Filipinos couldn't shoot very well. He stood up on the wall so he was visible from the waist up and would bob up and down waving his arms and yelling some unintelligible Jap words. I took a Browning automatic rifle from one of the soldiers and waited for his next move. He popped up and I let go a burst of three or four rounds. He flopped down on the wall and slid off behind it. I don't know if I killed or just wounded him, but a wild flurry of shots was directed at the spot where I had been.

The Filipino soldiers got a big kick out of the sniping and would laugh and yell at the Japanese in the fort. The Filipinos rigged up several large blackboards from the school and with chalk would write messages on them in Visayan (the Filipino dialect). These they put out at night and in the morning the Japs shot them full of holes. There were about 40 Filipino civilians in the Cota with the Japanese and they could translate the messages. We had several other tricks in the war of nerves. We made a number of long bamboo ladders and put them out where the Japs could see them. They wasted a lot of bullets trying to destroy those ladders so we couldn't attack the walls of the Cota.

We had a bazooka and nine shells we had received by submarine. One night we built a barricade by the road leading into the Cota about 150 yards

I look like I am posing in this picture but it does show the M3A1 .45 caliber grease gun that I liked to carry at that time.

away. The next day we fired several high explosive shells into the Cota gate, almost blowing it down. We could hear a lot of yelling inside and the Japs laid down a heavy fire at our lines for an hour or so.

We never intended to attack the Cota. The walls were about 30 feet thick at the base and about 10 feet thick at the top and about 30 feet high. With revetments along the top from which defenders could shoot, and with their 110 men the Japanese could hold off a much larger force and our casualties would have been very heavy, which we could not afford.

Our only hope was to get an air strike or to starve them out. We figured that the Japs had about three months' supply of rice and corn on hand. They also had a water well inside the fort. There was always the chance that they would make a break for it, but where would they go? The closest they ever came to doing this was send out a couple of soldiers with a civilian over the back wall to try and get to Cagayan by banca and to bring help. We discovered them and killed all three. From this we guessed that their radio was not working and we later heard from one of the civilians from inside the Cota that one of our first mortar rounds had knocked out their transmitter.

A Catholic shrine was built into the outside south wall of the Cota and regularly old women from town would visit it and leave flowers or a candle. We didn't bother them and the Japanese didn't either. This went on all during the siege up until the Cota was captured.

The siege lasted all of the month of November. During that time we kept the civilians that we had taken out of town concentrated in a school about four kilometers from town. We had several officers and men from the S-2 section detailed there to investigate them. We used some of the men for labor details and eventually released all but 12 who were actual collaborators. These 12 were sent to our permanent concentration camp at Paradise Valley in Lanao. All there were eventually to be tried by the Philippine government.

On December 5, I received a message from Colonel Bowler to report to his headquarters which had been moved down out of the mountains and was now at Maigo Lanao. Sinclair had already gone to the south coast of Mindanao to help operate two 26-foot whale boats sent to us by submarine. They were to help support Major Medina's 115th Infantry attack on the Jap garrison at Pagadian, Zamboanga. The whale boats were armed with bazookas and 20mm cannon in addition to small arms, and, acting as the guerrilla navy, prevented Japanese launches from traveling along the south coast from Malabang and Zamboanga.

We had captured some horses when we took Misamis, and Sergeant Bongalos and I left Misamis and spent the first night with Mr. Juridini at barrio Dimaluna, about 15 kilometers from Misamis. Mr. Juridini had been after me to visit him for some time, and he used to send me a bottle of native wine every week. He was a Spaniard and before the war had owned the bus company in Misamis. He had been very rich but the Japanese had taken everything. However, because of his nationality, they had not sent him to prison. He had a radio which he had been able to hide along with auto batteries to keep it running. He charged the battery with a combination of a truck generator, a bicycle and a Filipino boy. He kept us informed about the news. His house had running water and a flush toilet, although toilet paper had to be deposited in a bucket rather than clog up the septic system. That night I slept on clean sheets in a regular bed for the first time in about three years! Mr. Juridini had about seven servants, most of them nice looking Filipina women, and he served us Japanese beer and cigarettes given to him by the Jap commander at Misamis. We hated to leave, but the next day we got a sailing vinta with two boatmen and arrived at Maigo across Iligan Bay at 4 p.m.

Colonel Bowler was living with a Major Thomas, the chief of staff for A Corps, and they managed to make room for me. Rosi, the nurse who gave Bowler his asthma shots, was doing the cooking aided by old Zac, the cook who had managed to fatten me up when I first arrived at A Corps after the 17-day hike from Siokon. Colonel Bowler wanted me to come back to A Corps headquarters right away and be G-3. I managed to talk him into holding off until the fall of the Cota. I was expecting the air strike any day now and I didn't want to miss out on the victory.

Bongalos and I left Maigo late the next morning for Dimaluna. The Cota was built right on the beach at Misamis about 50 yards from the water. At that point Iligan Bay is very narrow, only about one mile across to the Lanao shore on the other side. On this return trip I decided to swing in close and have a good look at the Cota. I expected to stay at least 900 yards away, out of effective range of small arms. I must have misjudged the range. We were sailing along, still going in closer, when the Japs suddenly fired with an automatic rifle from the back of the Cota wall. The bullets ripped through our abaca sail and the two boatmen started to go over the side. Bongalos and I grabbed them and pulled them back, but they were so scared, they just huddled in the bottom of the boat. Bongalos grabbed the rudder and I grabbed the sail. We brought the boat around and headed away with the sail close hauled. The Japs were still firing and the bullets ripped through the sail and ricocheted off the water. We yelled at the boatmen to help us, but they were frozen with fear. The boat was about 20 feet long with outriggers and the wind was brisk. It was everything we could do to handle the boat, getting as much speed as possible and not capsizing. The bullets buzzed overhead like angry bees. Every once in a while I could feel one strike the hull. There was nothing we could do but pray. We only had a carbine and a .45-caliber pistol in the boat. Even if we had time to fire, we couldn't have hit anything from the moving boat. I expected any minute to be hit and, while holding the sail, tried to make myself as small as possible by lying along the bamboo slats on the outrigger poles. Bongalos wrestled with the paddle which served as a rudder and couldn't even duck. I kept saying to myself, "You damn fool; you damn fool." I had made some silly mistakes before but this was the dumbest I had ever pulled. It almost got us killed.

We finally sailed out of range and the Japs stopped firing. All during that time we never saw a Jap; they were calmly sitting down behind the wall, shooting at us as if we were sitting ducks in a shooting gallery. It was the most helpless position I have ever been in, even worse than in prison camp where my destiny was in someone else's hands. To make matters worse, it was all my fault for being there. Ever since that time I am uncomfortable on a small boat when there is a chance of action, because you just have to stand there and take it. Later, off Malabang in the armed whaleboat, I always felt exposed even though I knew we were more heavily armed than the Jap launches.

When we were out of range, Bongalos and I came about and took a breather. Now that we were safe, we both laughed from sheer relief. Bongalos had been with me for several months now, and we knew each other well, but now I felt like a brother to him. I knew he felt the same way.

We examined the boat and found seven holes in the sail and three in the hull. One had missed one of the boatmen by about two inches. We got the

A Moro sailing vinta like the one we were sailing when we came under Japanese automatic rifle fire from the Cota.

boatmen to work and proceeded to Dimaluna while Bongalos and I went over every detail. It seemed funny after it was over and those boatmen must have thought we were crazy. They wasted no time in getting home. Several times later I tried to get them to man a boat for me but they never would. I guess they were really calling me the "buang Kano."

Over barbecued chicken and fried eggplant, we told Mr. Juridini the tale. He laughed also, but I believe he secretly thought we were crazy. Mr. Juridini's cook always had something which we never tired of eating. He made crackers out of rice flour by frying them very crisp in a pan, then we spread butter made from carabao milk over them. Carabao butter is a cross between cottage cheese and butter and has a distinctive taste, I suppose because carabao milk is much thicker and stronger tasting than cow's milk. We spread papaya jelly to top things off.

We left early the next morning by horseback after a wonderful night sleeping on clean sheets on a spring mattress. We arrived in Misamis in a couple of hours.

The siege was dragging on and the soldiers were getting careless from inaction. The trench areas were in bad shape because, no matter how much I talked about it, the soldiers still threw trash around and didn't always dig a hole for a latrine. We were having quite a few cases of diarrhea and malaria and the flies were getting really bad. The soldiers just couldn't understand the American ideas of sanitation. If something didn't happen soon, we were going to have damn few men on the front line. A lot of men were AWOL because they hadn't seen their families in a long time and also simply because they were getting tired of the monotony. As long as there was some action, they were eager to work and fight, but when things became dull, they would get restless and think of home.

I felt much the same way and when I had a lot of time to think, I would think of home, my room, and my mother's cooking. Sometimes it was hard not to say, "Oh, the hell with it," and ask to be sent out by submarine. Whenever I felt like that, I would think of something exciting coming up, and I'd be off again.

We were also having a dog problem. Ever since we occupied the town, there had been a large pack of stray dogs roaming the town and hanging out mainly at the cathedral. They were messing up the cathedral floor and had become a real nuisance, barking at night and annoying the men on the front line by stealing food. We finally decided to eliminate the problem and over the next few days a picked group of men shot most of them and the rest disappeared.

We were following a regular daily routine of inspecting the front lines, checking on when we might expect the air strike, and pushing work on the airfield at Labo about five kilometers north of town. It was an old field built before the war but now grown over with small trees, bushes, and cogon grass. Colonel Fertig wanted to put it into operation so Southwest Pacific headquarters could use it for small planes and to resupply the guerrillas in western Mindanao. With the help of the mayors of the different barrios in the vicinity, we called on the Volunteer Guards and had anywhere from 200 to 1000 men working every day. Some of them walked 15 kilometers to work and received no pay. We did buy up a few demijohns of tuba once in a while and gave it to them.

Bonilla and I went out to the field on horseback every two days. We had several lieutenants in charge of the work and our trips were as much to keep up the people's interest as to inspect the condition of the field. We were still waiting for an air strike on the Cota which was to come at any time now.

On December 11, Bonilla and I were sitting in town in the 3rd Battalion headquarters having dinner when we heard some planes fly over. This wasn't unusual as planes had been flying over almost every day and some had even circled the town with the appearance of taking pictures. This was probably in preparation for the strike. When the planes began to circle fairly low, I went to the window to look out. Seven P-38 Lightnings seemed interested in the Cota. The P-38 is a long-range fighter and possibly came up from Morotai. Bonilla and I dashed down the steps and as we hit the street, we heard the first burst of machine-gun fire and could see one of the planes pulling up from a run on the Cota. By this time all the troops knew what was happening and they yelled, cheered, and danced around in the streets. The planes made runs on the Cota, firing 20mm and .50-caliber machine guns into the wooden buildings inside.

I grabbed my Tommy gun, jumped on the old rickety bicycle that I had gotten from the Japs, and headed down through town to the front lines. The soldiers in the front line also yelled and cheered as smoke began to rise from the Cota. The incendiary bullets had set the wooden buildings on fire. The planes made their runs from north to south and consequently all misses went out into the water as planned.

The Cota burned fiercely now. The planes finished their strafing and circled to see what was happening. After a few minutes, they buzzed the town, wagged their wings, and flew off to the south. The whole inside of the Cota was burning and the big wooden door looked like it was beginning to fall in. We could hear the Japs yelling inside the Cota. Their ammunition began to explode. We also heard the steady crackle of small arms bullets and the dull explosion of mortar shells or grenades. Several Japs had jumped over the wall and were crawling toward several old bomb shelters in front of the Cota. We had a lot of fun picking them off. Every now and then, one would stagger to his feet and run; there would be a flurry of shots until he fell down.

The buildings inside the Cota began to fall in and the fire was dying down a bit. Bonilla and I called together our assault units with their ladders and got ready to storm the walls. We couldn't go in the gate as it was choked with burning timber. We could see that the main damage had been done to the inside front and the south sides of the Cota. The buildings on those sides had completely fallen in while the buildings on the north and back side of the Cota were relatively untouched by the flames, although they were riddled with bullet holes. We had no way of knowing how many Japanese were still alive so we set our assault for about 5 p.m. The fire had died down and we had units with ladders ready to assault on three sides, covered by fire from our front lines.

As the ladder units started forward, the Japs began a scattered firing, but quickly the fire became heavy. Evidently the Japanese were still operational in good strength. Our units had to pull back. We had a few casualties and the ladders were left out in the open field. We saw how easy it was for a few men to defend those walls. The Spaniards knew what they were doing when they built the Cota against attacks from the Moros.

Bonilla and I decided to wait until night to probe forward again. The Japs continued to fire more than usual, I guess to let us know that there were still plenty of them left. The Japs were usually very conservative with their ammunition, but now they laid down a heavy fire on our front lines.

Bonilla and I were at the 3rd Battalion headquarters at about 9 p.m. when we heard a series of mortar explosions down at the Cota. We were out of mortar shells and this was the first time the Japs had used theirs against us. It was pitch black outside, and we headed down the middle of the street toward our front lines. Mortar shells were exploding all along our front lines. The Japs were laying down a heavy curtain of rifle and machine gun fire. Red tracers ricocheted off the street and buildings and lit up the night sky.

The soldiers were nervous and wondering what was happening and we passed the word by runner to lay low in the trenches and keep an eye out for any Jap movements out of the Cota. The Jap fire wasn't doing much harm, but it certainly made everyone keep his head down. We worked our way around the perimeter, reassuring the troops and directing some fire back at the Cota, but we could see no Japs in the dark.

At about 10:30 we heard a lot of yelling and firing from our lines on the north side of the Cota. The firing had died down everywhere else and I wondered what had happened. A runner came in panting and wet with mud. He said the Japs had gone over the rear wall near the water and had crawled through the thick underbrush of the swamp on the north side. There was a mangrove swamp there that was waist deep in water most of the time. H. Company had strong points on some of the high ground.

Under cover of darkness and behind the heavy diversionary firing, Japs had gotten into the swamp and headed north along the coast, probably to pick up a boat and try to escape by sea to Cagayan across Iligan Bay. We estimated the force to still comprise about 80 to 100 men. We sent one more company in addition to H. Company after them and advised the guard company at Jimenez by telephone to be on the alert for them.

At 1 a.m. our troops picked up 40 civilians in the swamp who had come out of the Cota also. We sent them back to the prison compound under guard for questioning. They were in a terribly starved condition and some were wounded. One little girl about 18 years old had her left arm badly burned and had shrapnel wounds in her side and leg.

At daybreak our patrols engaged the Jap force at Jimenez. The Japs had gotten two large sail boats and were traveling up the coast. Some of our soldiers put out in a boat with Browning automatic rifles and Thompson submachine guns and were able to drive the Japs toward shore. When they were close in, our soldiers sank one of the boats which drifted ashore. The Japanese soldiers we either shot in the water or they drowned. Our soldiers recovered a .30-caliber machine gun from the boat, set it up and, using the ammunition from the boat, turned the gun on the other boatload of Japs. After a short exchange of fire, where we had the great superiority, the Japs abandoned the boat and tried to swim away. Fifteen were captured and the rest were killed or drowned.

All during the fight the people living in houses near the beach had gathered and insisted on watching the fight and cheering. They were warned about the danger but paid no attention. Our only casualties were two of those civilians killed by rifle fire from the Jap boat. Unfortunately one of the casualties was the wife of one of the soldiers taking part in the fight.

We went into the Cota at first light. The ruins still smoked and we found 20 dead Japs and 3 wounded. Two of the wounded were so far gone that I ordered one of the lieutenants to put them out of their misery. He fired one .45-caliber bullet into the temple of each one. The third had shrapnel wounds in his knee and could not walk. He looked terrified as the other two were shot but soon realized that we were going to spare him. The Filipinos wanted to kill all of the prisoners, but we had orders to take them alive for intelligence purposes. We eventually called in a C-47 to Labo field and sent them all out to higher headquarters.

Inside the Cota we found the graves of six civilians who had been killed by our mortar fire. Five sacks of corn and a small, frightened carabao were left in the Cota. If the planes had not come, the Japs could not have held out much longer. We found parts of the radio, a little medicine, and five cases of ammunition. Later, out of the burned debris, we recovered 86 burned rifles, a lot of helmets, bayonets, mess kits, canteens, and two burned officers' sabers.

Up on the top of the Cota walls we found three Japanese soldiers who had committed hara-kiri. One had put the muzzle of his rifle in his mouth and with his toe on the trigger had blown out the back of his head. The other two had clutched grenades to their stomachs and pulled the pins.

During the engagement at Jimenez, when the Japs saw that they were finished, they dumped their knee mortars and automatic rifles overboard. We never recovered them. We later learned that a boatload of about eight Japs got to the Lanao coast but were captured by the troops of Colonel Hedges' 108th Division. At the end of the campaign the guerrilla forces had captured 26 Japs and killed 79. On our side we lost 16 men and had about 25 or 30 wounded. Some days later we learned via radio that MacArthur's headquarters announced the liberation of Misamis Occidental Province by the forces of the Tenth Military District and that this was the first province to be liberated in Mindanao. I felt pretty good after hearing that!

13. Reorganizing Guerrilla Headquarters

I WAS now supposed to proceed immediately to A Corps headquarters at Maigo to assume my new duties as G-3, but Major Bonilla scheduled a going-away party for me on the night of the 13th in the municipal building. Mrs. Capistrano and all of her W.A.S. girls attended. We had an orchestra made up of boys from the regiment. Where they found the drum, sax, trumpet, and banjo, I can't imagine, probably from a Chinese merchant in the hills. The W.A.S. girls served coffee and cakes. Of course there was a demijohn of fresh tuba to pass around.

The dance was the typical rural Filipino one where the girls all came with their parents and sat on benches on one side of the room. The fellows all sat on the other side and when the music started, they went over and picked out a partner, returning her to her seat when the dance was over. The only way to see a girl alone was to arrange to meet her outside for a few minutes. At the right time she would excuse herself to go outside, then you would take your chance and step out in the dark to meet her. A lot of that was going on.

On the morning of December 14, 1944, Bongalos and I went by vinta to Maigo, the new headquarters of A Corps. The next week we spent getting a house fixed up and establishing the new office for the G-3 staff. A family in Maigo kindly let us use their house while they moved in with relatives.

A few days later Colonel Hedges came down from his headquarters at Iligan and advised that he was going by launch to Dipolog on an inspection and asked if I wanted to go. I thought as G-3 that I should go along. Anyway, I wanted to see the country. At that time, Colonel Hedges was chief of staff of A Corps and commander of the 108th Regiment located in Lanao. He had come down from the hills in October when the Japs had retreated from Iligan to Cagayan. This was at about the same time that we had attacked Misamis; Colonel Hedges had since rebuilt most of the bridges and repaired the roads all along the north coast of Lanao. He had three trucks and three automobiles in operating condition, all running off alcohol. The vehicles had been hidden on the far side of Lake Lanao by American officers when the islands surrendered and had been kept hidden from 1943 until December, 1944. Colonel Hedges brought them across the lake on bamboo rafts and put them in running condition.

We were to go to Dipolog in a 30-foot, wooden sailing vinta, with outriggers, and fitted with a V-8 engine which enabled us to cruise at six knots. The hull was five feet wide at the top and about five feet deep. Platforms extended across the hull and out on the outrigger support poles. Our party included Colonel Hedges, myself, Major Gillon, who was going over to take charge of the Dipolog airfield, and six guerrilla soldiers. We carried a supply of alcohol for the engine, two Browning automatic rifles and some standard rifles. We flew the American flag. This was necessary because our planes were patrolling the area and anything not flying an American flag was fair game. We still had to watch out for Japanese planes which were still patrolling too. We kept a sharp lookout.

We left Iligan on December 26, and on the way we crossed Iligan Reef which rises to about eight or ten feet off the surface of Iligan Bay. I could see the dark green shadow of the reef. The waves occasionally broke into white caps as they rolled over the reef. We made several passes over the reef with hooks and lines out and caught five or six *talaketok* up to about 15 pounds. That night at Plaridel on the north coast of Misamis Occidental, we had a good fish dinner.

The next morning the weather looked threatening, but we started out anyway. The weather spared us until we got to Punta Blanca on the north coast of Zamboanga. The sea is always rough rounding that point and with the wind blowing like it was, we were nearly pounded to pieces. One of the poles supporting one outrigger broke and several of the guy ropes running from the top of the mast to the outriggers snapped. We were taking the sea over the side and everything and everybody was soaked. We managed to keep the motor running by covering it with canvas, but the boy operating it nearly passed out from the alcohol and exhaust fumes. Once we got around the point, things got better and we could repair the broken pole and lines. As a safety precaution, I had tied my bags to the boat so I wouldn't lose them if we capsized. I had learned from past experiences!

We arrived in Dipolog about 5 p.m., and proceeded to Colonel Garma's headquarters to meet him and his staff. "Nick," the American guerrilla running the radio station there, had a house and we moved in with him. His Chinese cook Ah-Kee turned out good food. Some American planes had been dropping in to the airfield, thus he had some canned goods to work with. It was funny: the crews coming in wanted fresh stuff—onions, eggs, chickens, bananas, papayas, fish—while we wanted canned goods, Spam, corned beef, sardines, dry biscuits and stuff like that from home. This made it easy to barter to everyone's satisfaction.

We remained in Dipolog over New Year's Day, making an inspection of the 105th Division and setting up some .50-caliber machine gun defenses around the airfield. Several Japanese planes had been over lately and we wanted to be ready for them if they attacked the field.

We had a small party on New Year's Eve, organized around several bottles of "whiskey" given to us by Mr. Uriquaga, a Spanish Basque living at barrio Sicoyac on the beach north of Dipolog. The whiskey was made by triple distilling tuba. It made a really good drink with citrus juice and raw sugar. Mr. and Mrs. Uriquaga served us a huge baked fish covered with homemade tartar sauce made with eggs, coconut oil, vinegar, and seasonings. It was a memorable New Year's Eve party.

We left Dipolog on January 3, 1945, and spent the first night with Mr. Barica at Baliañgao Zamboanga. The next day we sailed around the north coast of Misamis and at about 4 p.m. tied up at the pier at Jimenez and walked the two kilometers up the hill to town and the "casa" of the Ozamis family. The family, headed by Doña Carmen, owned a large coconut plantation along the coast but had been living in the hills during the Japanese occupation. They had recently moved back into the house after we had liberated the province. Some Japanese officers had used the house, but it was not damaged too much. It was much like home, with working shower and toilet, and inner-spring mattresses with sheets and pillows. The food was cooked American style, and we all ate sitting at a huge banquet table seating at least 10 or 12 and served by house boys and girls. Their home-cured ham was almost as good as Virginia hams. During my stay in Misamis Occidental, I made many 20-kilometer trips either by foot or horseback up to Jimenez to enjoy their hospitality. They had extended an open invitation. The evenings of conversation or cards were always so enjoyable.

We arrived back in Iligan on January 5 after a pleasant trip across Iligan Bay. The weather was perfect without a cloud in the sky. I got a good suntan while I spent the trip experimenting with an air-sea-rescue sunstill making fresh water out of salt water. As usual with a tropical tan it faded in a few days out of the sun. Using one of Colonel Hedges' cars, I got back to Maigo and A Corps headquarters the next day. My assistant, Lieutenant Eviola, had been in charge while I was away. I really didn't like the routine of an office and my idea was to travel around and see things first hand and personally direct any operations that needed to be done. I felt like a stranger when I was back at HQ and I let Lieutenant Eviola handle the paperwork.

Shortly thereafter Colonel Hedges came down and asked if I would like to help him inspect the Moro troops up at Lake Lanao. I jumped at the chance and was off again. Major Blow was in charge of the Maranao Militia Force (Moro troops) of the 108th Division and was going to meet us at Dansalan on the Lake. Lake Lanao is in the center of the province of Lanao and at an altitude of about 2000 feet, cool enough at night to require a light cotton blanket. The Moros around the lake grow Irish potatoes and lettuce which varied the diet a bit. The Japanese had maintained a garrison there but had pulled out because the Moro guerrillas gave them so much trouble, ambushing their truck convoys and rolling big boulders down the cliffs to close the road.

Before the war there had been a Philippine army post called Camp Keithley at Dansalan, and we were now using those wooden buildings for division offices and barracks. There was also a small airfield that would barely permit a C-47 to land. The field sloped sharply down to the lake and the planes had to land uphill and take off downhill.

Colonel Hedges had sent word that he wanted all Moro units to assemble at Dansalan for inspection and registration of arms. Most of the arms in the hands of the Moros weren't accounted for, and we needed to get them on record. The Moro troops were being paid at that time with our guerrilla currency and as an inducement, the word was passed that every man who registered a gun would receive all of his back pay. It was necessary that we have a count of the arms so they could be collected or kept account of after the war. Otherwise, the arms would fall into the hands of bandits and cause trouble as had happened before the war when there were a number of armed bandit groups scattered around the province. Most of the guns were Philippine Army Enfield .30-caliber rifles and, as a general rule, no newer arms had been or were being issued to the Moro troops. Many of the Moros had *baltiks,* or homemade guns. These were made from three-quarter-inch water pipe. Twelve-gauge shotgun shells just fitted them. The pipe was fitted into a larger pipe so it would slide back and forth. A wooden stock was put on the opposite end of the large pipe with a short length of nail sticking up in the center of the larger pipe. A hole was cut in the side of the larger pipe. The small pipe was slid forward, a shell loaded into it, the gun was pointed at the target, and then the small barrel is jerked sharply back. The nail hits the primer of the 12-gauge shell, and the buck shot is on the way. At close range it's a deadly weapon. There were also a few replicas of the army rifles with handmade barrels, hammers, triggers, and ejectors made to fit the .30-caliber cartridge. Those Moros who didn't have rifles carried barongs, krisses, and *campilans;* some even carried spears. Every Moro man carried a fighting knife of some kind stuck in his belt. I believe the Moro valued his knife or certainly his rifle more than his wife.

One of the datus at the lake had a 2.95 mountain artillery piece left over from the Insurrection of the early 1900s and had a cache of about 100 shells. However, the cannon didn't have a firing pin. He fixed that by placing an iron pin in the hole in the breech and fired it by hitting the iron pin with a wooden mallet. It worked! Needless to say, he was a very influential datu around the lake area.

After the inspection and registration of arms, the Maranao Militia Force marched in review around the parade ground. One thousand warriors in their multicolored mailong and headdresses, their unit pennants waving on bamboo poles alongside the Stars and Stripes, made an impressive and

Moro knives presented to me: Left: Old wavy kriss given by *datu* Salila at Siokon and my only weapon until I got to A Corps headquarters. Third from left: Ivory handled, silver mounted wavy kriss given by *datu* Macarambon at Lake Lanao. Right: Moro Barong given by a *datu* at Iligan City, Lanao. Small dagger: Silver mounted dagger given by *datu* Bushwan Kalaw at Maigo, Lanao.

stirring as well as unusual sight as the brass agongs kept time to the marching.

We went down to the market by the lake after the parade was over. The merchants had their goods spread out on banigs and were selling everything from vegetables, hand-woven cloth, brass vessels, and agongs, to bells, bracelets, knives, and Moro jewelry. I bargained for a couple of knives with silver mountings made from old Spanish coins. I still have them hanging on the wall in the den. The bargaining took some time, as the price always starts out very high and it's up to the buyer to haggle it down. I got so that I enjoyed bargaining. The merchants would argue, plead, or even cry, pointing out how poor they were and asking, "Have pity on me only, sir!" My cue was to stand fast or start a sob story of my own. After the deal was completed, I learned never to feel sorry for the seller. If the bargain was too hard, the sale would not have been made. The merchant always made sure of a good profit.

We spent two days at the lake, then returned down the hill by car past the beautiful Maria Christina Falls (later to be incorporated into a hydroelectric plant after the war), and past the burned out PT boat beside the road. This boat American and Filipino forces tried to take up to the lake before the surrender. It was one of those that brought MacArthur to Mindanao from Corregidor for his flight out to Australia.

Arriving back in Iligan was like getting back to civilization, with its electric lights and water system. We were staying in the officers' quarters, and Mrs. Mercer, the widow of a Filipino officer, was the manager. Her cooking was American style and was a welcome change from the usual native fare we got out in the hills. I must admit, however, that I had not forgotten the two and one-half years of prison camp food and I always enjoyed the native food and especially some of the unusual items like octopus, fresh water prawns, wild pig, and *salegupons* (locusts). Eating was always an adventure on Mindanao.

Back in Maigo the next day, I settled down to the dull life of making reports and answering communications. Maigo was just a wide place in the road about 60 kilometers from Iligan. The only excitement was listening to the radio at Bowler's house every night or drinking tuba in the "Victory Cafe," which was a nipa shack in the barrio, lighted by coconut oil lamps. In every barrio there seemed to be a "victory cafe." Later in Misamis when A Corps moved back, it was the "Victory Garden" and included a girl playing the piano. Over tuba or tuba wine, Simmons, Mooney, Douglas, Coe, Thomas, and I used to sing all the old songs we could remember, much to the delight of the crowd inside and those gathered around outside also.

The availability of food in Lanao was getting to be a problem. With much better facilities in Misamis, Colonel Bowler decided to move the headquarters back over there. Misamis was a much larger town and food was

Some of the boats used in the "Guerrilla Navy" along the coast of western Mindanao. Note the American flag to prevent our being strafed by U.S. planes.

easier to get from the countryside. For the move we contracted all the large bancas and vintas we could find as Misamis was only a three hours' sail away.

I decided to go over on one of the large sailing bancas with Bongalos and four or five of our guerrilla soldiers. It was a clear day and the wind pushed us along at a steady speed. Several of the boys dipped up a couple of large jellyfish, discarding the milky veins and parts. The clear jelly was cut up into cubes about one inch in diameter and put in a coconut dish with some lime, vinegar, and crushed chili peppers. This sat for about an hour then the "cooks" passed it around. I couldn't resist and took some. It tasted like it looked: a piece of jelly soaked in hot sauce with a faint taste of fish. The Filipinos assured me that this was the best for vigor and energy. I had it several times later on vinta trips, but I didn't notice much added vigor.

We were sailing along about half way across the bay. I was lying out on an outrigger taking a sunbath with the cool water splashing over me when

Opposite: Becky, Miguela, Rose, and Moro friends at Maigo, Lanao, in January, 1945. The ladies are wearing mailongs, the Moro equivalent of sarongs.

suddenly three Corsair F4U fighters popped up over the hills of Lanao, dropped down to water level, and made a run over us. I knew our planes were ranging around the island, looking for Jap launches, and my first inclination was to dive under the water to escape their fire. Instead I scrambled back to the boat and yelled to the crew to get out our American flag. By this time, the planes had pulled up, turned, and were coming back on another run. The boys got the flag out. I guess the pilots saw it and a white guy in shorts standing on deck waving his arms, because they didn't fire, came back on another pass, wagged their wings, and flew away. It was then that I discovered that I had lost my VMI ring in the scramble back to the boat. It had been loose on my finger and now it was gone after surviving two and a half years on a string around my waist in prison camp!

It was February 5, 1945, when we got back to Misamis. Major Bonilla, who still had his headquarters there, had a house picked out and cleaned up for us. Sinclair was back from the south coast and was in the process of fixing up a number of old launches he had found in different places around the bay. He planned to add these to the "Guerrilla Navy." Simmons was in town with his radio station and we all three moved into the house. It was a large two-story, wooden house with a tin roof and koa shell windows. With spare equipment from the radio station, Simmons had rigged up electric lights. We had an artesian well in the yard, so we could pump water into the house. Each of us had a separate upstairs room. We had a large living room and a covered porch. The house was now completely furnished with items loaned to us by Mr. Juridini. We had a wooden hot tub, built by the Japanese, out in the side yard. We could have a hot bath out there at any time with water heated in a bucket over an outdoor fire. We had a Chinese cook and each of us had a "boy" to clean up, handle laundry, and wait on the table. The local Filipina women would do our laundry. Food could be bought at the village market which was operating again since people had moved back into town. Things were really getting "State-side."

The other Americans lived in houses scattered around town. There was a central mess hall where we usually ate also. Labo Field was already in use so we were getting an occasional shipment of supplies from Leyte. The first plane to come in was a PBY Catalina to test that the runway was satisfactory. After that, C-47s also were used. We also had an emergency landing. A P-38 Lightning ran low on gas and had to land. He barely made it as the field was so short. We had some gasoline flown in and he managed to take off OK after a rev-up.

We kept busy for the next couple of weeks, getting the headquarters straightened out and operating and getting some antiaircraft machine guns

Opposite: The house occupied by Simmons, Sinclair and me in Misamis, February, 1945. Note Japanese "hot tub" at the side of the house under the shed.

set up at the field and in the dock area. The Volunteer Guards were repairing the roads and working on the town water system. The Japs had torn out a lot of the pipe, but we managed to get running water to part of the town.

One morning we heard a plane approaching and went out to look. It was a Jap fighter flying low over the water and headed down the bay. In a little while the sound ended abruptly, and we sent a runner to find out what happened. He was back in a few hours to say that the pilot had ditched his aircraft at Dimaluna right off the beach from Mr. Juridini's house. I got a horse and proceeded to Mr. Juridini's at a gallop. When I got there, the pilot was being held by some of our soldiers. He had come ashore with his life vest and parachute which was hanging up to dry. The plane, we were told, was offshore and about 200 yards. I decided we would try to raise it. The next morning I got two big sailing vintas and went out to look at the plane. Some oil slick was visible, so we started diving to locate it. We shortly found it in about 20 feet of water, resting right side up on a soft mud bottom. We got a line around the tail section and, with the two vintas, pulled the tail up to the surface. However, that was all we could do. We didn't have enough flotation to raise the whole plane. I dived down several more times and managed to get the gun sight out of the cockpit. The plane was in good shape, but we had to let the tail go. Later I advised the Navy that it was there and could be easily salvaged. They appeared interested but nothing ever came of it. I guess they were too busy elsewhere to send a salvage vessel, or maybe the water was too shallow for them to get to it. They did want the pilot, however, for G-2 to question, so we sent him out by plane in the next few days. Mr. Juridini wanted the parachute, which was silk. I gave it to him on the condition that his girl would make me a pair of pajamas. She did and I still have them.

The town was growing all the time. New nipa houses and *tiendas* (stores) popped up everywhere. The public market was going strong, and we soon had to put out a price control list to stop the profiteering that was starting. At first, this didn't work too well, but after the MP's arrested a few people, things got a lot better. Of course, there was also a black market starting, and we had to keep close tabs on supplies which were being flown in to us. A bar of Palmolive soap would buy a girl; and it was one of the items that we kept under close control.

Major Thomas and I had met a couple of American-Filipina mestizo girls while in Maigo, and we decided to pay them a call. They lived in Maranding Lanao about four hours' sail on the other side of the bay. The weather looked

Opposite: From the left are Lewis, Simmons, Thomas and Wills at Labo Airfield where civilian guards are unloading a C-47 with supplies from Leyte, February, 1945.

good on the Friday that we started out at 2 p.m., figuring to be there for supper. We had a small sailing vinta carrying a crew of two and Thomas and me. Everything went along fine. We sailed past Juridini's house and continued up the bay. About halfway there a sudden squall blew in. We had to lower the sail and ride it out. Between the rain and the waves breaking over the boat, we got everything wet including the cigarettes we were taking to Becky and Miguela. When we finally got ashore, we discovered that we had a four-kilometer walk on a muddy trail in the rain.

We arrived about 9 p.m. to find everyone asleep. We were two of the saddest sights ever seen when we got inside the house. We didn't have any extra clothes, so we had to borrow some while ours dried over the fire. We sat up until about 12 a.m. drinking coffee and talking, but we were two of the most unromantic looking guys in the world with shirts that wouldn't button and pants that were about three sizes too small – and no shoes. I think that seven-hour trip to Maranding would rival anything a frontier Romeo ever did!

Back at headquarters in Misamis, life went on as usual, with our main efforts directed on getting out intelligence information to higher headquarters concerning Jap troop movements and air activities over Mindanao. We now had good radio contact at all times. We also rushed work on the roads, bridges, and telephone system. We now had in operation a road running from Dipolog, Zamboanga, all around the northwest coast of Mindanao past Iligan to Manticao, Misamis Oriental, a distance of almost 220 kilometers. The bridges were made of coconut logs and had to be repaired continuously. Our telephone line now reached from Misamis to Dipolog and from Iligan west to Maranding. A line to connect these two was under construction, but it was a 24-hour job just to keep it working and, of course, we had the old crank type magneto phones.

Sinclair had several launches working and with the four that Hedges had, we maintained a good launch service between Misamis and Lanao. Besides all of this, we were sending supplies to the other guerrilla divisions in Bukidnon, Cotabato, and Zamboanga, where our guerrilla forces were putting the pressure on the Japanese garrisons. As G-3 for A Corps, which included all of western Mindanao, it was my responsibility to plan and coordinate our operations in that area.

Opposite: **Thomas (right) and I with one of the bombed-out cars we repaired and had running on cane alcohol.**

14. The Malabang Campaign

THE middle of February we decided to open a campaign against the 400-man Jap garrison at Malabang on the south coast of Lanao. We wanted to prevent the Japanese from using the airfield there. We had also received a request from MacArthur's forces to furnish them with certain data about the coastal waters and the terrain in that sector. Colonel Hedges was to furnish the troops for the operation. Major Blow was to conduct the operation. Captain McClaren and Lieutenant Sample with some troops were to set up supply bases. About 400 well-trained guerrilla troops were available and about 1,000 Moro warriors would be on call for the operation. Jock McClaren had a 26-foot whale boat armed with a 20mm cannon to patrol the coast. The whale boat had been sent up to us by submarine and had a one-cylinder diesel engine mounted amidship. Not having diesel fuel, the engine ran on coconut oil. It worked fine once we heated the engine head with a torch so the coconut oil would flash!

I was going along to coordinate the operation. Bongalos and I left Misamis on March 2 and went overland by Lake Lanao. I chose that special route because I wanted to see more of the Moro troops, and I wanted to visit our radio and coast watcher station located in the hills of Lanao overlooking the south coast and Illana Bay. We had been observing Jap launch traffic in and out of Malabang for some time. We had a large spotting scope and could observe the town of Malabang about 15 kilometers away.

We went by launch to Iligan and spent the night with Colonel Hedges and had a good meal at Mrs. Mercer's officers' mess. Colonel Hedges had a car waiting the next morning and we drove up the hill to the Lake. Besides Bongalos and me, several couriers traveled with us, carrying messages to the units on the south coast. The Christian troops seldom made the trip across Lanao without an American along as the Moros would not give them any assistance at all, and there was the possibility that a Christian Filipino would just disappear!

At the lake I met my good friend *datu* Binasing Macarambon. His wife was sick with malaria so I gave him a course of atabrine for her. He insisted on presenting me with a magnificent wavy kriss with a silver and ivory hilt. (It is now the most prized knife in my Philippine collection; see photograph on page 126.)

We transferred to a large Moro canoe about 25 feet long with outriggers and an outboard motor. On the way across the lake, we stopped at Tugaya where the Moros make a lot of knives and jewelry. Before the war it was seldom visited by outsiders because of the uncertain attitude of the people. I had Captain Aguam and Lieutenant Kiram, both sons of an influential datu, with me so there was no danger to our party. One sobering note, however, was a human head hanging from a mango tree as we walked into town. Aguam told me that the head was taken in an interfamily feud by a man in Tugaya from a family across the lake. As an added insult, the head had been hung in the tree for everyone to see. He told me that everytime the "taker" passed, he shot at the head for practice. It did have some holes in it!

Tugaya was built by the lake and the old stone mosque was surrounded by a wall and had its own fish pool inside. The houses were spaced around the mosque in no certain pattern, but each was surrounded by a fence of sharpened bamboo stakes, thus forming a kind of cota, or fort. Some barriers were more elaborate with fences of stones. We talked to the datu for a while and watched a shopkeeper casting brass bowls in a sand mold. The people were friendly enough and all were happy that we were going to attack Malabang. Many of the men from the village were going to be in on the fight.

We pushed on to Ganassi on the south coast of the lake and the deputy governor of Lanao Province, *datu* Miguel Alug, insisted that we stay in his house that night to visit with him, his wife, and his nine-year-old son, Abdul. His was a typical Moro house of wood with carved and painted beams and posts and surrounded by a rock fence. In his bedroom *datu* Alug had his sleeping place padded with two 2-inch-thick slabs of rock so no one could shoot him through the walls or stab him with a spear through the floor. The house was built on posts which raised it six feet off the ground. Datu Alug was an educated Moro and had a daughter about 17 years old who had been going to school in Dansalan before the war. After dinner she, Abdul, and I played Chinese checkers until 11 p.m. Abdul was the big winner; I never won a game.

There were no beds in the house. Our hosts spread grass banigs for us to sleep on. At some time during the night a number of shots were fired through the roof of the house by someone out in the dark. The next morning Datu Alug explained that some rival datu fired the shots to prove to Alug that he could still shoot at his house even if he did have some American officers visiting him! Such rivalry, or *maratabat,* went on constantly between the various datus.

Datu Alug loaned us horses, and we started for the radio station at Gas, about six hours' ride away. Our baggage was carried by Moro cargadores, and we had a guide furnished by *datu* Alug. As a rule Moros will not carry anyone else's baggage, being too proud to be used as "beasts of burden," but in this case, they made an exception. We traveled a well-worn trail for about three hours, passing through Moro farm land in the rolling country surrounding the lake. Cultivated fields and houses surrounded by fences were everywhere. The houses were always on the top of hills, half concealed by bamboo clumps, enabling the occupants to observe visitors before they arrived. At Lake Dapiak, Alug and his son turned back, and we cut off through the forest on a foot trail. The horses could barely make it in some places, and instead of our waiting for them, the cargadores had to wait for us.

The forest teemed with monkeys and birds and the trail was a tunnel through the dense vegetation. Once in a while we would pass through an old *caingin*, or open field grown up with eight-foot-tall cogon grass, the blades of which are serrated and sharp and can give a nasty cut. I passed the time asking Bongalos questions about the birds, trees, and anything else I could think of. He was used to this. He always had an answer. I learned a lot about Filipino life and customs from him during our days in the guerrilla.

We arrived at Gas at 11 a.m., but it took another hour to get to the radio station. Gas is supposed to be a barrio, but is spread over five square kilometers, with only 15 houses, one on every other hill top, each just like the other, made of bamboo and cogon grass and surrounded by a little clearing planted in corn and comotes with a few chickens and a dog or two. Gas is a very poor community. We passed the datu's house and the only thing that differed was that he had a horse and owned a pistol. He was very friendly, but I don't believe he had ever had a bath. He was extremely proud of his nickel-plated .38-caliber revolver.

We arrived at the radio station and after a few hellos, I gave Watson and Knudsen their mail which had recently arrived in Iligan. It had been sent over from Agusan by Colonel Fertig. A submarine had brought in some supplies and with it some mail. I was anxious to get a look at Malabang, so while the men were reading their letters, I went down to look through the telescope. I could see the whole south coast of Lanao from Ibus Island all the way east to Parang Cotabato. No ships or launches could pass without being observed. With my naked eyes I could see the landing field at Malabang and the red roof of the old Spanish fort and the watch tower in town. Through the telescope I could see the Jap watch tower at the field and the big acacia trees around the buildings. While I was watching, I did see two figures walk up to the tower and then go back under the trees again. It could have been the guards changing. Those Japanese didn't know it yet, but pretty soon they weren't going to be using that tower anymore!

Our attack on the garrison was set for March 6, and until that time all troops were cautioned not to make their presence known in any way. Except for a few small reconnaisance patrols, no troops were to approach the airfield until the attack order was given. B-24 Liberator bombers were being sent up to soften up the town. They were supposed to hit on March 6 or 7. Our troops were then supposed to move in.

At the radio station we had rice, mongo beans, and monkey meat for supper. We had arrived just a day too late as the officers had already finished off a wild pig given to them by the Moros. The monkey wasn't that bad; it had been boiled first, rubbed with garlic and then roasted. We had some native coffee, but the supplies of dried fish and raw sugar had not yet arrived from the coast. I had planned to spend the night at the station, but the cargadores were anxious to either return home or go on to Ramain down on the coast where Rex Blow had his headquarters. No other cargadores were available at Gas, so we had to push on. Ramain was four hours' hike away but downhill most of the way. The trail and terrain were much like what we had passed through in the morning, but there were a few more people. Very few white men had been down in this country, and whenever we passed a shack, everyone came out to stare, not smiling or frowning but just wondering. We waved and smiled but they just continued to stare. This was poor country. The people were all dirty and half-naked. I didn't see any carved and painted houses like the ones around the lake. We met some men and women coming up from the coast carrying coconuts in baskets hung on poles across their shoulders. I wanted to buy a couple to drink, but they gave them to us and would not take any pay. We squared up the deal by giving each one a fresh American cigarette.

We got into Ramain in time for supper. I was certainly glad to get off that little horse and that wooden saddle. I'm sure the horse was even more glad to get me off. I still wonder how those little horses do it. They are only four to four-and-a-half feet high, but they can travel all day at a fast shuffle, even with a big American on board.

The soldiers had built shacks of bamboo and cogon grass under the coconut trees. Major Blow had a house about 15 feet square. We had a big meal that night, all sitting around a little table about three feet square. Major Blow, Captain McClaren, Lieutenant Samples, Major Silva, Captain Tabiquero, myself, and three other Filipino officers ate a meal centered around a couple of cans of corned beef washed down with pure alcohol mixed with evaporated milk and brown sugar which resulted in something like a milk punch. When that gave out we dropped back to the old standby, tuba.

An old datu had insisted on coming down to take part in the coming fight. He was about 65 or 70 and was the father-in-law of *datu* Alug in Ganassi. His name was *datu* Lagindab. He claimed to have 23 wives! He sat down with us most of the time but, of course, as a Moro, he couldn't drink any alcohol. He had a .45-caliber automatic and needed some cartridges. I traded him a dozen for six ornate gold-plated buttons for a woman's blouse. My wife still has them today, several made into earrings.

We had a lot of work to do the next day so we turned in early. We had to gather all the data about the coast, the airfield, and the off-shore soundings and send it back as quickly as possible. We decided to divide the job up. Blow was to take the soundings off the beach, McClaren was to cover the beach south of Malabang. Samples was to cover the beach north (east) of Malabang. I was to cover the airfield and surrounding territory.

We all slept in the one little house. After we all got our mats down, no one could get out without falling over someone's mosquito bar. I don't know why some of us didn't sleep outside. The house was about five years old and the roof was practically eaten up by bugs. When it rained, we had to stretch our ponchos over our mosquito bars to make our own little tent inside the house. I was so tired by the time we went to sleep that I never gave a second thought to the hard floorboards. I did wake up in the morning with a numb ear from pressing against the floor all night.

We all got away early the next morning. I had 15 men, all armed, in my group. The Japs still patrolled the field and there was the possibility that we could run into them. It was about two kilometers to the field. We approached from the northwest through the coconut groves. Just before we got to the field, we sent a man up a tree to see if he could see anyone moving around. He reported no one, so we moved on to the field. It was a large field with two runways at 90 degrees to each other. The largest ran from the beach back toward the foothills. Aircraft parking areas were located off the runways under the coconut trees, areas now grown up in bushes and small trees. Except for the longer runway running north and south, the rest of the field was grown up in cogon grass about three or four feet high with footpaths trampled through, no doubt by the Jap patrols.

In the first parking area, we found some fresh boot tracks, clearly showing hobnails, which could only mean Japs. The tracks had been made the previous afternoon or earlier in the morning. It made me a little more cautious, so I sent five men with a non-com around to the north end of the field to keep a lookout while we went on to the south end at the beach and crossed over into the parking area on the other side. If the Japs detected us and tried to come around behind us, they would engage our lookouts and warn us. We scouted the parking area and crawled through the tall grass across the field several times. We traveled in single file, and I was expecting to run into a Jap patrol at any time. I was just nervous enough to keep my tommy gun cocked all of the time. We covered the whole area and didn't see a soul.

We found the wreckage of several Jap planes and parts of parachutes that came off our para-frag bombs. We found an unexploded bomb, but let it lie. We picked up our outpost at the north end of the field. One of the soldiers pointed out what he said was a Jap lookout. To me it looked like a bunch of leaves in a tree, but I took out my glasses and he was right. A Jap soldier was in the crotch of a tree on the other side of the field. He had probably seen us, but it didn't make any difference now. We had gotten the information we wanted.

We got back to camp at 3 p.m. I was so thirsty I drank three green coconuts *(batoong)*. I didn't own a canteen. Whenever I wanted water, I got Bongalos to get me a couple of batoong. The liquid was always cool and a big coconut yielded nearly a quart.

We were lying around camp resting at 4 p.m. when we heard some firing down toward Malabang. The rest of the teams got back at about 6 p.m. The launches had gotten into a little excitement. Blow had taken McClaren down to the south side of Malabang by launch and left him, then went to take soundings off the coast. He picked up McClaren at 4 p.m. and as they passed the beach in front of Malabang, they were fired on by the Japs. The launch returned the fire with the 20mm cannon and the Browning automatic rifles and the firing from the beach stopped. On the way home they discovered three bullet holes in the boat.

Everyone was tired enough to check in early after supper. I didn't wake up until 8 in the morning. I usually woke up around 5 a.m., so I had to be really tired to sleep through to 8.

We didn't have much to do that day. We sent the data on the coast back to Colonel Hedges by runner. The B-24's were supposed to start bombing that morning, so, after breakfast, we all went up to the top of a nearby hill to watch. A big crowd of Moros had gathered, and they could hardly wait to see the fireworks. Several times planes passed in the distance, and we could hear explosions somewhere up the coast, possibly at Malangos or Pagadian where Major Medina was supposed to have the Japs under siege. By 10:30 we were beginning to wonder, but decided to wait a little longer. The Moros were getting restless. We heard some planes in the distance. They seemed to be coming our way. We could see two groups of six planes each, and they were B-24 Liberators flying in beautiful formation directly for Malabang.

The Moros went crazy, jumping in the air and waving their krisses and barongs and yelling insults at the Japs. Five kilometers away the two groups of planes separated, each flight approaching at a 90-degree angle to the other. They seemed to be floating through the air. They passed over the target three times without dropping any bombs. We began to think it was just a reconnaissance flight so we were going to have a lot of explaining to do to the Moros. The planes came back on another run and a great shout went up from the soldiers and the Moros. Then we saw it: a steady stream of black objects rained down from the planes. The planes held their course, then started a long sweeping turn out to sea.

The explosions began. We could see columns of red dust and smoke rise from the acacia trees, then we heard the dull pounding of the explosions.

From the dust we could see that the bombs were hitting right along the road that ran from the airfield to the town. Most of the Jap troops were bivouacked along that road. The first explosions had hardly died down when the second flight came and dropped their bombs on the town. The bombs hit exactly on the spots that we had indicated on maps sent to the air force several weeks before. We could imagine the Japs looking up to see those big planes flying over, seeing the bomb bay doors opening, and then watching the bombs hurling down to the place where they were trying to bury themselves in the ground. The same thing had happened to me at Clark Field and on Bataan; now I had the satisfaction of seeing the same thing happen to them. The planes swung away and headed for home. The smoke and dust cleared away and we could see several fires had started in town. The planes hadn't touched the airfield; it was going to be used when our forces made a landing.

Back in camp I got a radio message from Thomas asking me to get back to headquarters as soon as possible. I was to come back by Pagadian and set up a defense along the road to Misamis as they expected the Jap garrison at Pagadian to try and come up that road into Misamis. If the Japs managed to break through Medina's thin line around Pagadian, they would threaten our operations in Misamis. McClaren said he would take me by launch to Tukuran near Pagadian and if we left by 3 p.m., we could be there by 9 p.m. As we were loading up the launch just off Ibus Island, a Moro paddled up in a vinta and wanted to trade a beautiful Moro dagger. We finally settled on a pair of my khaki pants and a khaki shirt. The dagger had an ivory bird's head handle and a full silver hilt and case. (My wife and I used it to cut our wedding cake in 1946.)

Just after we started up the coast, 12 Corsair F4U fighters dive-bombed and strafed Malabang. We could see them go into their dive then pull up just before the explosions. I hated to leave just when the fun was starting, but orders were orders.

Our troops launched their attack and, after making initial gains, they put the Japs under siege. The planes returned daily to bomb the town, and our troops finally moved into the town. A number of Japs were killed, but the rest escaped to join the garrison at Cotabato City. Our campaign to free Malabang and the airfield took about 20 days, and when our American forces landed at Malabang in mid–April of 1945, there wasn't a Jap within 80 kilometers.

The trip up the coast was uneventful. Several times a little to our discomfort, one of our planes would drop down to have a closer look, but our flag satisfied them and they left us alone. Later it began to rain and the sea got rough. If we weren't taking water over the bow, our screw was whirling in the air. The big 20mm gun made the boat bow heavy, so we had to all get in the stern to keep the bow above water. We kept the hand pump going to pump out the bilge. In the darkness the coastline all looked the same. The place we were going was about 10 kilometers east of Pagadian. I was afraid we would go right past and end up in the Japs' lap at Pagadian. Jock was sure he knew where to go, so I kept my worries to myself.

We did get to Tukuran, and when we ran up in the shallows and waded ashore, there wasn't a soul or a light in sight. It was still raining, but there was supposed to be a guard on the beach. We walked up to the little group of shacks that made up the town and beat on several doors before we finally found an old man and his wife who told us the soldiers had all left when they heard the boat, thinking it was the Japanese! As there was only a squad of soldiers, they thought it best to get out of town. Even the Volunteer Guards and most of the civilians had evacuated. We rounded up some of them and made them stand guard on the beach the rest of the night. Jock got something to eat and started back for Malabang, by traveling all night he expected to be back before dawn. It was safer to go at night as even with the flag, it was risky traveling in the daytime. Some trigger-happy Corsair pilot might shoot first and look later.

I hung my wet clothes near the kitchen fire, rolled up in my poncho on the floor, and went to sleep. The next morning Bongalos rounded up the soldiers and got them back on their post. We got some Volunteer Guards as cargadores and started for Aurora about 20 kilometers away through the forest. The dirt track went up into the hills. It was a steady climb all of the way. We passed some large teak trees, so I tested the leaves to see if they could be used as sandpaper as I had been told. They could. Later we passed a large durian tree with fruit on it and some ripe fruit lying on the ground. I could smell the fruit long before I could see it. Durian has a smell somewhat like Limburger cheese, but the spiny fruit is full of delicious tasting, custard-like meat. We ate our fill and pushed on.

At several places along the road I marked places for defense positions on my map. We arrived in Aurora about lunch time and got hold of Lieutenant Lugtu, the company commander there. We worked out a defense in depth with units from his company covering all trails coming from the south. When the Japs moved, they had a habit of marching in two or three columns, the main body coming up the road with flank units moving up trails parallel to the main route of march. My idea was to put out small units on all approaches from the south with our main body held at a convenient place to the rear. When the forward units contacted the enemy, they were to send runners back. The main body could then move in any direction to attack the main body of the Japanese. The soldiers prepared foxholes and automatic rifle positions along the trails that could be used when needed. The Japanese never did come up by way of Aurora, but finally evacuated Pagadian by banca and small boats to Cotabato City.

From Aurora we could return to our Misamis headquarters by three different ways. I could take the road north and hike to Misamis, a distance of about 90 kilometers, or I could hike to the bay and take a vinta to Misamis, a trip of about 12 hours, or I could take the road east toward Iligan as far as Kolumbugan, then take a vinta across the narrow bay to Misamis. A truck from Colonel Hedges was at Aurora and was returning to Iligan. I decided to go with them to Kolumbugan, a distance of 60 kilometers.

We left Aurora in midafternoon, traveling the first 20 kilometers in low gear as the road went up and down steep hills. We didn't have any brakes and the only safe way was to travel so slowly that we could shift into reverse so we could stop in case of an emergency going down hill. My heart was in my mouth for those first 20 kilometers. The coconut log bridges didn't have any guard rails and every time we crossed one, which was every few minutes, I could feel the bridge shake and tremble. If one of them had collapsed, we and the truck would have rolled down the deep ravines hundreds of feet below, stopping, I'm afraid, in a crumpled mass of wreckage. I could lean out the door and look down on the tree tops below. In addition, the bridges were so narrow that the wheels were riding on the edge of the logs. Many times, due to a sharp turn, we had to back up several times before we could get all four wheels on the bridge.

We came out of the mountains and the rest of the road to Kolumbugan, about 40 kilometers, was at sea level, and we could make good time. I insisted on stopping at Maranding to see Becky. We had a cup of coffee before pushing on. The dirt road was so torn up that by "good time" I mean we could average about 20 kilometers an hour. At Kolumbugan, Bongalos and I grabbed a sailing vinta, shoved off, and hauled up the sail. The wind was blowing briskly and the waves were fairly high, and, in addition, the tide was running out. The combination of the two made for a rough passage. We finally had to lower the sail for fear of capsizing in the sudden gusts of wind. Normally in a strong wind, men can stand on the windward outrigger which will be out of the water and have no trouble climbing in and out to balance the boat. But with strong gusts of wind, no one can move fast enough and it's easy to capsize. We had our gear tied to the boat in case we did turn over, but for safety, we paddled the rest of the way across. At one point we passed over a coral reef very close to the surface with waves five or eight feet high rolling over it. We had to wait, catch a good wave, then paddle madly across. We finally arrived at Misamis, March 10 at 10:30 p.m., tired and soaking wet. I got so I hated to cross that stretch of the bay because every time I did a big blow would come up.

It felt good to be back in Misamis and "home" as I called it. When I went to the old Spanish building that served as headquarters for A Corps the next morning, I found out why I was called back so quickly. Colonel Bowler was expecting a visit from Colonel Fertig and also a shipment from Leyte was coming in by boat. I had ordered a lot of demolition equipment so we could step up our sabotage work around Zamboanga City and over in Bukidnon along Sayer Highway. We were very short or out of TNT, time delay fuses, primer cord, and land mines. As soon as we could get a supply, we could send them out to the units in those places and they could further disrupt the Japanese truck traffic. Our planes patrolled the roads, but at night the Japs could still use the roads. In addition to demolitions, we were getting a 37mm antitank gun, a couple of 75mm mountain howitzers, and some more bazookas of the folding type. We also had ordered a quantity of self-igniting paper, exploding fountain pens, and booby traps to be sent to Zamboanga to be planted in town by our agents. It was my job to pick out some men and show them how to use these items.

On the morning of the arrival of the cargo boat, we had everything ready down on the dock. The supplies were coming by LCI (landing craft infantry) and it was due at 8 a.m. A channel had been sounded and marked so the boat could come in. We had an unloading crew of about 100 soldiers standing by. The LCI arrived on time with a small gunboat escort. When they docked, we had gangways and the crew ready. They wanted to unload as quickly as possible as there was still the danger of Jap planes, and the LCI was at a disadvantage tied up to a dock. The crew kept their gun manned all of the time and their radar working. We had a 20mm Swiss Orlikon anti-aircraft gun mounted on one end of the dock and had three .50-caliber machine guns mounted at different points in town. Nothing happened, however, and we got everything unloaded by 11 a.m.

Sinclair and Simmons were feeling right at home back on a Navy vessel. After showing us around, one of the officers took us down to the wardroom and we all had breakfast: bacon, eggs, toast, jam, and good old American Navy coffee with cream and white sugar. This was really a treat! What we did enjoy more than anything else was the ice water. There was a cooler right outside the wardroom and we couldn't keep away from it. Before we left, we had a chance to go down and buy some cigarettes and candy bars from the ship's store. The last thing I did as I was leaving the ship was to take a long drink of that water cooler.

We were sorry to see them pull out. Before they left we had some of the soldiers go into town and collect fresh vegetables for them. We gave them onions, eggplant, bananas, coconuts, and fruit which was about all they really wanted. Of course some of the sailors traded cigarettes for native hats and bolos. The Filipinos learned in a hurry how generous the sailors could be and drove hard bargains. The sailors caught on soon after, however, and weren't averse to driving a hard bargain themselves. When the boat pulled out, I think everyone was satisfied with his "deal."

After the boat was gone, we were very busy for the next few days moving supplies into bodegas and making up lists of what was to be sent where. They had brought a Jeep also, the first I had ever seen, with a trailer which we put to good use.

On the left, my house on the edge of town at Misamis. This building was a former bus station and had a large number of garages. The road to Jimenez is on the right.

I had moved into a house of my own out on the edge of town. Bongalos had rounded up a lavandera to do my laundry, and Connie had moved down to Misamis with the hospital group. We saw each other quite often. Life was really enjoyable. We were also getting some supplies by plane at Labo field and these had to be distributed also. Officers from the different divisions scattered around the island came into Misamis to collect their supplies and take them back by launch, banca, and cargadores, which took a long time to the more distant units. On all future deliveries we made arrangements to have them delivered direct to the other parts of the island by plane to guerrilla airfields or by Navy vessels. All of our supplies were coming from 8th Army so we had only one headquarters to go through.

The commanding general for 8th Army was going to the States on leave, so he left his B-25 Mitchell bomber with us to use. It came in to Labo field, and the first trip we made was to our secret airfield at Farm #2, constructed by Major Thomas with Subano labor in north central Zamboanga in the vicinity of barrio Dipalo. The field was contructed and then camouflaged with movable nipa shacks, false logs, and foliage.

We took off from Labo, Captain Davis the pilot, Colonel Bowler, Major Thomas, Major Kingsbury, and I. It was a short flight to the field and after making a pass over the field and seeing the obstructions removed, we

Our B-25 was like this one but had fourteen .50-caliber machine guns firing forward. I sat in the navigator's seat behind the pilot.

dropped down to land. Davis thought the field was a bit short as we were coming in at about 130 miles per hour; he lowered full flaps and we touched down doing about 100. I was sitting in the navigator's seat and looking through the top bubble or over the pilot's shoulder. The length of the field ahead of us was decreasing at an alarming rate. Davis was braking and braking as much as he dared. When we finally rolled to a stop, the nose wheel ran off the compacted runway and sank about a foot in the soft mud. We all piled out to see the damage. Luckily we were only stuck in the mud, nothing broken.

A large group of Subanos had come out of the surrounding forest and after they looked around, we put them to use. Under the direction of the guerrilla soldiers stationed at the field, we loaded as many Subanos as we could as far back in the fusilage as they could be squeezed. Then, using all of us and the rest of the Subanos, we lifted on the front end and the nose wheel. Slowly the nose wheel came out of the mud and we all rolled the plane backwards until the nose wheel was on the hard surface. Cigarettes were handed out to the soldiers and the Subanos. We loaded up for the take-off. Davis revved up and swung the plane around; with brakes full on he warmed up the engines, ran up to 200 rpm until the plane was straining against the brakes, he then released the brakes and we were off to a jump start. Speed picked up rapidly and just as we reached the end of the runway, Davis pulled the plane up and we were away. I could hear everyone relax.

We swung out over the Sulu Sea looking for any possible Jap launches. The plane had fourteen .50-caliber machine guns firing forward and we were dying to use them. We flew down the coast but didn't see anything. We turned back, flew across northern Zamboanga to Iligan Bay and touched down back at Labo. It had been an interesting flight. (Later at Dipolog I was to use the plane again.)

Back in Misamis the routine of the G-3 office continued. One afternoon when I got to my house, I was very surprised to see Vicenta Gondamon waiting for me in the living room. I had not seen her since the incident at Semata when I left Camp X. She had not changed and was still a striking young woman with her long black hair and really magnificent figure. I didn't want to get involved, but she told me she just wanted to get some clothes to take back to the Subanos at Semata. Bongalos and I gathered together his and my spare khakis (we could get some more later). We had five or six pairs of pants and shirts. I told her we could round up some more the next day. She asked if she could stay in the house overnight. I agreed as I figured she didn't have any close friends in town, and we had several separate rooms. We ate in that night and turned in early. The next morning Bongalos dug up some more clothes, and Vicenta was on her way back to Semata. A puzzling woman, she seemed more Polynesian than her Filipino-Malay heritage. I never saw Vicenta again.

15. The Dipolog Campaign

COLONEL Fertig came to Misamis in early March from his head-quarters on the other side of the island and started a reorganization of the island command. Instead of having two corps (A and B) under the 10th Military District, he organized all commands directly under the 10th Military District, which took in the island of Mindanao. Colonel Bowler, commander of A Corps, was going to be liaison officer to 8th Army in Leyte, and Major Thomas left for the States. I was appointed G-3 for the 10th Military District and promoted to major as of March 20, 1945. The new headquarters were to be at Dansalan on Lake Lanao. Colonel Fertig was leaving immediately for Dansalan, and I was to follow later. Just before he left, Colonel Fertig told me he had a job that he would like for me to do. One of our airfields was at Dipolog and the Japs had sent up a force of about 150 Marines from the city of Zamboanga to try and take the airfield from us and to try and shut down our treasury at Dapitan, Zamboanga, where all of our Mindanao emergency currency was being printed. Up to this time more than 9 million pesos had been printed, and it was the money on which the guerrilla organization depended: it paid the troops and bought supplies from civilians. The Jap force was closing in on Dipolog in spite of everything that the local troops could do. I was to reorganize the forces and wipe out the Jap patrol.

At that time our forces had been using the Dipolog airfield frequently. Our forces had landed at Zamboanga City on March 10, 1945. That landing was being supported by Marine Air Group-12 with Corsairs flying out of Dipolog. Two companies of American soldiers from the 24th Division in Mindoro had been flown in to set up a perimeter around the town to prevent the Japs from interrupting our use of the field. These troops were being withdrawn as they were needed back on Mindoro. We were going to have to stop the Japs with our own forces.

Before leaving for Dipolog I had a lot of things to do in Misamis as I would not be coming back, but would go to the new headquarters at Dansalan. An unusual event occurred the next morning when a pretty, young Filipina *dalaga* (girl) about 16 years old, with an older woman who I supposed was her mother, showed up at the house with a note from Mr. Juridini. The note informed me that he thought I needed, to put it in his words,

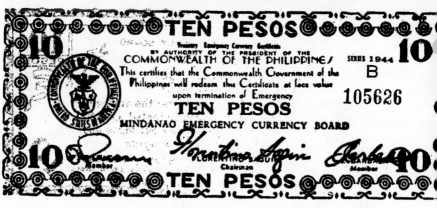

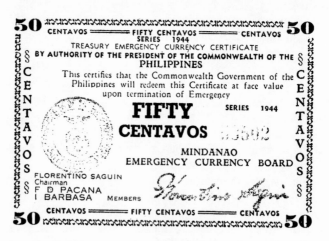

At the top is a sample of Japanese occupation currency. The other two notes are guerrilla money printed by our treasury at Dapitan.

"a concubine, and the bearer of this note will assume that position in your house." I sent them back to Dimaluna with a note refusing his offer but thanking him for his consideration. Mr. Juridini's offer wasn't that surprising; he had a couple of mistresses of his own around Dimaluna, and I guess he thought that I, being single, needed some feminine companionship. Actually the practice wasn't that unusual in the Philippines, as many businessmen had girlfriends living in apartments or houses conveniently located to their places of business.

Bongalos and I gathered together a good supply of ammunition and medicine to be given to the 105th Division troops at Dipolog under Colonel Garma, as I knew they were short of everything. Colonel Bowler loaned me the Jeep, and we loaded it and the trailer with everything it would hold. We had a .50-caliber machine gun and an 81mm mortar with several different kinds of ammo, high explosives and white phosphorus. We also arranged for the Jeep to return and bring over the 75mm mountain howitzer. The road to Dipolog had just been opened. This would be the first trip over it.

We left one morning at about 11 a.m. I didn't know it at the time, but this would be the last time I would see Misamis until after the war as a civilian.

The trip to Dipolog was uneventful. We made it in two days with a stopover at Mr. Barica's house at Baliangao. His house was built right by the water, about 200 yards from the concrete pier. Again we slept in real beds, but with rattan webbing, no mattresses, but with clean sheets. The toilet even worked when you flushed it with a bucket of water. We ate a good meal of beef in the dining room at the table with all the family. It really seemed civilized.

Baliangao Bay (or Murcelegos Bay) is a beautiful natural bay surrounded by a tropical paradise of coconut groves growing down to the beaches. In some places rocky cliffs come down to the water. The bay is full of coral reefs and heads with a ship's passage leading in to the pier. The shallow waters of the bay shade from blue to turquoise to green and brown. A few small islands are scattered in the bay and in the Diupu River which feeds into the bay. The strange sea mammals called *dugongs* (manatees) are still found here, as well as a multitude of marine life: giant rays roll up to the surface and from the pier, I saw a school of banded sea snakes swimming by. Wading in the shallows, I turned over a piece of coral and caught two baby octopus. We walked over to the coast of the Mindanao Sea to the north and passed a tree full of giant fruit bats (flying foxes). Since it was almost dusk, they were squealing and scrabbling around, ready to take off for the night's feeding on jungle fruit trees. We were careful not to walk under the tree for we would have been showered with urine. All the vegetation under the tree was burned by it.

Early the next day we left Baliangao and arrived at 105th Division headquarters early in the afternoon. Colonel Garma, whom I had met before in July of 1944, and again in December, 1944, when Colonel Hedges and I visited Dipolog, was there as was Major Bonilla, who had been sent over from Misamis to assume command of the troops to be used in the operation. I also met the American Major Marcy, who commanded the two companies of American infantry that had established a perimeter around Dipolog and the airfield. I learned that we would have to act fast as the Americans were being flown out on either March 27 or 28.

Our patrols had determined that the Japs, located 16 kilometers from Dipolog, were armed with two knee mortars, a light machine gun, two automatic rifles, and approximately 100 rifles, and were still on the move, approaching Dipolog from the southwest. The Japs were still located in the hills 8 or 10 kilometers in from the coast. The area was forested with only an occasional isolated settlement. It was from these settlers who were running away from the Japs that we were able to determine where they were.

In planning with Major Bonilla, we assigned units to take up the positions of the American Infantry when they pulled out, and we organized a force that we would send into the hills to attack and pin down the Jap patrol. Captain Encanardo with reinforcements had arrived from Misamis and would be part of that force. Also, Colonel Hedges was sending over a picked group of 100 Moro warriors under Captain Sumpio. The Moros were to arrive in a couple of days by LCI. These two units would bring our forces up to about 500 men and their previous experience at Misamis and Malabang would give a morale boost to the local troops.

Over the next few days we were busy moving the units around and sending the other units into the hills to contact the Jap force. Captain Sumpio arrived, and we beached the LCI south of town and moved his men into the hills. The airfield was still being used by Marine Air Group 12 to support our troops who had landed at Zamboanga City on March 10. There was a lot of traffic on the small grass landing strip. Gasoline, armaments, and other supplies for the planes had to be brought in, in addition to supplies for the infantry companies, which included rations, medical supplies, and ammunition. At any one time there were F4Us and C-47s parked on the strip.

Shortly after I arrived, there was a tragedy at the airfield. Returning from an air strike on Zamboanga City, two of the Corsairs landed too close together and the second in line ran up on the one in front. The propeller chewed the front plane up to the cockpit. The pilot was killed. A C-47 was called in to fly the body out and also the other pilot, who was in complete shock from inadvertently killing his friend. The incident threw a pall over the town for two days.

The wreck of the two Corsairs blocked the runway, so some of the boys and I spent all night blowing the two planes apart with plastic explosives

NR 2 GR 60 010944 NO 13 ———————— RCVD 011410
BEGINS CLN BRIEF REPORT RECEIVED FROM TMS CONCERNING YOUR CON
FERENCE WITH HIM PD YOU HAVE BEEN DESIGNATED GEORGE THREE FOR
DISTRICT PD ISSUE WRITTEN ORDERS FOR ATTACK AND IF THEY ARE NOT
FOLLOWED PREFER CHANGES PD RELIEVE BONILLA IF HE WILL NOT RPT
NOT GIVE YOU HIS FULL SUPPORT PD ADVISE PARA TMS TO PASS
CONTENTS TO GARMA PD

A TRUE COPY:

     For ~~POBILUYKO~~
                INF FRS
       JOAQUIN F. UZOA
          CPL INF
     CHIEF CODEMAN, FRS

5 April, 1945.

Major Donald H. Wills, Cav.,
Dipolog, Zamboanga.

Dear Major:

    I was well pleased to receive your message this morning stating that
it appears the boys are beginning to fight. Major Thomas radioed me that
Captain Encarnado with his men have arrived. Captain Gil Sumpio, who has been
with Major Blow at Malabang, is being sent with 100 picked men. Captain
Sumpio has been instructed to report directly to you for orders. His unit has
tommy guns, but no BAR's, and it is suggested that some of Encarnado's BAR's
be transferred to Sumpio's company. It is hoped that these reinforcements,
small as they are, will be sufficient to liquidate the pocket of Japs.

    We are landing a small quantity of supplies for your use. Additional
supplies will be flown to you as they are needed. There will be few luxury
items, but we will supply basic food and ammunition.

    Once you have the enemy surrounded, I suggest that you obtain his
surrender. I am anxious to finish this matter, and it would be much simpler
if you could persuade them to surrender. The enigma of this whole affair is
why did the Japanese patrol ever attempt to reach Dipolog? My personal opinion
is that they are actually cleaned out from Zamboanga, and faced with the
attack, they ~~were enroute~~ to Dipolog, which they supposed to be in their hands,
    [there traveled]

    Hq Eighth Army is sufficiently interested that they will send a
plane in to pick up any prisoners that you may capture.

    In closing, I repeat that you have my best wishes for the early and
successful completion of your mission. You are needed here to complete the
District Staff.

                Sincerely yours,

                      WENDELL A. FERTIG
                      Colonel, C. E1.
                      Commanding.

Top: Radio message from Thomas advising of my appointment as G-3 of the 10th
Military District on Mindanao. *Bottom:* Letter from Colonel Fertig advising of
the 100 Moro troops being sent to beef-up our attack on the Japanese position
at Dipolog.

from Major Marcy's supply, so we could drag them off with our old truck onto the beach out of the way. The beach was beginning to fill up with wreckage. A few days earlier a P47 Thunderbolt had crash-landed on the beach when the pilot couldn't make the field.

Our troops in the hills had contacted the Jap force and had pinned them down on a thickly forested ridge about 8 kilometers from the coast. We moved in six companies of the 107th Regiment on the ridge just to the south of the Jap position and Captain Sumpio's Moros to the ridge just to the north of their position. Our 75mm howitzer was moved into position and, using observers with field telephones in the units in position around the Japs, we could register hits on the ridge occupied by the Japanese.

Now that we had them pinned down, I decided to arrange an air strike on their position. Before doing so, however, I wanted to go up there and see the situation for myself. Bongalos and I took the trail up the Tangian River and, in a couple of hours of climbing into the hills, arrived at our troop position. The Japs were on a forested ridge about 500 yards away across a deep gully. I wanted to have a closer look, so I borrowed a pair of glasses from one of the Filipino officers of F Company and jumped into a fox hole on the forward side of our ridge. The fox hole was built of coconut logs stacked to create a three-and-a-half-foot wall to get behind and with a coconut-log roof overhead. Crouching in the hole, I studied the opposite ridge with the glasses. I had been there a couple of minutes when all of a sudden I came under sniper fire from somewhere. Several bullets smacked into the coconut logs. Needless to say, I ducked into the bottom of the fox hole. I had not seen anything and didn't know where the shots were coming from. I yelled to our troops, but they hadn't seen the source of the shots either. After a few minutes, I told them to put down a covering fire, and I jumped out of the hole and back over behind the ridge. Now I knew the Japs were there. I got on the telephone and set up an air strike for the next morning.

At about 2 p.m. Bongalos and I started to hike out. I wanted to get back in a hurry to be sure everything was arranged. We made the trip in about an hour. The day was terribly hot and by the time we got down to the road, I was soaking wet with sweat and I collapsed under a coconut palm. I was dizzy and so weak I couldn't stand up. I figured "heat stroke." Bongalos brought me several green coconuts and after about an hour in the shade, I began to feel better. I telephoned the troops on the front line and told them to mark their front lines with colored plastic panels. When we got back to Dipolog, I confirmed that the strike would be the next morning on March 27.

The next morning I met Major Blanchard at the field. He had four Corsair F4Us warming up and armed with 500-pound bombs. We didn't have any photos of the area and no maps on which to mark the targets. Having just been to the area and being familiar with the terrain, I suggested that I would get in the lead plane, the pilot could sit on my lap, and we could

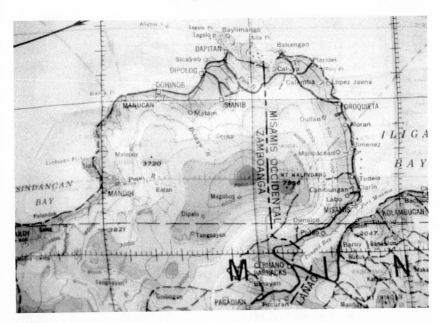

Section of a silk survival map from the Army Air Force showing the area of the
Dipolog Campaign.

guide the strike in. Major Blanchard agreed, so Lieutenant Sharp, the
smallest of the pilots, sat on my lap. We couldn't put on parachutes because
there wasn't enough room. We loaded up and took off. We flew the short
distance down the coast to the mouth of the Tangian River, then we swung
inland. In a few seconds we were over the target and could spot the markers
of our front line troops. We made several passes over the area while I
pointed out the ridge where the Jap positions were. Then, leading the other
three planes, we made a run over and dropped our bombs. We pulled up,
watched the explosions, then proceeded to make a number of strafing runs
along the ridge using our .50-caliber ammunition. We couldn't tell much
about the effect as the vegetation was very heavy on the ridge, but we did
see several areas start to burn. We returned to the airstrip, loaded up with
ammunition again, and made another strafing run over the target.

Moving into the area the next day, our troops found that our strike had
made a direct hit on the Japanese bivuoac area. We had killed 60 Japanese
and the men gathered up a lot of abandoned Jap equipment. The survivors
had divided up into several small groups and headed back into the mountains. Our job was to now pursue those groups and eliminate them. The next
day one of the Filipino officers presented me with a Jap officer's sword and
one of their battle flags, picked up in the area.

We had relieved the pressure on Dipolog, the American Infantry

"AIR-GROUND COORDINATION"—2dLt W. C. Olsen and 1stLt W. S. Sharpe demonstrate the method used to carry Major D. H. Wills, AUS, leader of Dipolog guerilla forces, as he directed Marine Corsairs against jungle-hidden enemy positions.

A Marine Corps photo made after the action showing how the pilot, Lieutenant Sharp, sat on my lap in the F4U Corsair for the strikes against the Jap positions. We did not wear parachutes as there was no room in the cockpit.

companies had been withdrawn to Mindoro, and our units could now control the situation. When the Americans pulled out, Major Marcy was kind enough to leave his supplies of plastic explosives, medicines, and K and C rations with us. They were put to good use by our troops. I must say that some of the plastic explosives somehow ended up in the hands of some of the civilians, because days later I heard some dull explosions down by one of the inlets. I went down to investigate. Some fishermen were using plastic explosives to make a harvest of fish. They would shape a piece into the size of a baseball, put in a cap and fuse, light it and toss it into the water. The stunned fish would float to the top where they could be gathered in. While I was there, one of the charges didn't go off, so the fishermen just dived down, recovered it, brought it ashore, loaded it with a new fuse and tossed it in again. Kind of dangerous work, but I left them alone as I knew they needed the fish.

Captain Sumpio and his Moros were pulled out, loaded on launches sent over by Colonel Hedges, and sent back to Lanao, but not before we loaded them down with U.S. Army rations, cigarettes, and extra khaki uniforms.

We still had some SBD-Douglas Dauntless dive bombers using our airfield, and I was able to borrow them on several occasions in the next few days to search for the Jap stragglers. Riding in the rear gunner's seat and

An SBD dive bomber like the one we used for the strikes against the Japanese forces at Dipolog. Ours was marked "4th Marines" and I manned the twin .30-caliber machine gun in the rear seat.

acting as navigator and spotter, I led a number of flights back over the area to try and locate the Japanese. We were carrying bombs and on one occasion we spotted a group in a clearing deep in the forest. We bombed the clearing but couldn't check on the results. Another time I spotted a group of about 10 men beside an abandoned nipa shack in a clearing. They were dressed like Filipinos and when we flew over at tree top level, they waved at us. I couldn't see any guns in evidence and because there was a faint chance that they might be Filipinos, we didn't fire on them. Back at Dipolog I found out that none of our troops were in that area and that there was no one living in that area. We hopped in the plane and flew back to the clearing, but of course they were gone. I was to learn later that the Japanese stragglers often dressed like Filipinos to escape detection.

On the return to the airfield the pilot was making his approach to land, and I was about to unbuckle my safety belt, when the pilot suddenly applied full throttle and the plane rolled over! We couldn't have been more than 200 feet off the ground. I waited until we touched down and the plane came to a complete halt before I unbuckled my belt. Getting out, more than a little shaken, I told the pilot how close I was to having no safety belt on during the victory roll!

"No matter," he assured me, "even unbuckled you would have stayed in the plane. The centripetal force would hold you there." Nevertheless, in the future, I waited until the plane stopped before I unbuckled.

A lot of traffic still used our airfield. Our B-25 Mitchell had come over and was at our disposal. General Eichelberger had sent us an L-5 observation plane for Colonel Fertig and the Colonel sent it over for me to use. One day a C-47 landed and one of my classmates from VMI, Phil May, stepped out. I think he had been shot down, rescued, and was being returned to his unit. We shot the bull for awhile.

A B-24 Liberator had landed to refuel and offered to take a bunch of Filipino soldiers up for a ride. As we cleared the field and swung out over the water, one of the Filipinos pulled a lever and deployed the life raft over the side door. There was a horrible noise and the plane lurched violently. The pilot came around fast and landed. The life raft had blown back and hit one of the tail surfaces, damaging it severely. It was lucky that we got back. The B-24 sat on the field for the next week or so, waiting for a new tail assembly and mechanics before it could return to base.

Things were running smoothly. The Jap stragglers had disappeared, broken up into small bands, in hiding, or trying to find their way to some safe area – and there weren't many of those left.

We used the B-25 to range up and down both coasts of Zamboanga looking for targets. We wanted to use those 14 guns firing forward. I would sit in the navigator's seat behind the pilot, and we would fly at about tree-top level. We flew past Coronado Point where I had come ashore from the prison ship, and I even saw the little beach where I had landed. This was really fun, and I was having the time of my life. In my letters home (sent out with accommodating airmen), I told my family I was safe, would be home soon, but wanted to stay just a little while longer.

One day we did try out the .50-caliber guns on the B-25. Spotting an abandoned nipa shack along the road on the west coast of Zamboanga and flying at tree-top level, we let go a burst of 12 guns: the 8 nose guns and the 4 package guns. The plane slowed down about 40 knots and the nipa shack disappeared in a cloud of dust and debris.

The L-5 observation plane with the pilot, Captain Kellet, was also an ideal way to range up and down the coast and across the Mindanao Sea, past Aligbay Island and up toward Negros looking for Jap boat traffic. Aligbay Island was a small, low, coral and sand island boasting a few coconut palms and bamboo clumps and a population of Moro sea gypsies *(Sajug)* living in huts on poles over the water. Most of them were fishermen, but there were also some Moro pirates living there who preyed on small sailing vessels using those waters between Zamboanga, Negros, and Siquijor Island. We had not had any trouble with them, however. I sat in the back of the L-5 with the door flap down. I usually carried an M-3A1 .45-caliber submachine gun (grease gun) and a box of hand grenades. One day as we flew out northward toward Aligbay Island, we spotted a sailing banca and dropped down to have a look. We were about ten miles off the coast. There were 11 men on board, all dressed like Filipinos, and as we flew past at water level about 50

An L-5 like the one we used to sink the boat-load of Japanese soldiers trying to escape to Negros from the Dipolog area. Ours was an Army plane and was painted olive-drab.

feet away, they waved. I didn't see any guns in evidence but they could have been hidden down in the hull. We pulled up, made a steep turn, and dropped down for another swing past. They had seen the gun sticking out the side window and I guess they panicked. Five of them jumped overboard. We pulled up and on the next swing by, I could see a white cloth with a red sun in the middle floating in the water. They were Japs and one of the soldier's good luck belt of a thousand stitches had come off. When I think back and realize what sitting ducks Kellet and I were in that little, slow L-5, I know "someone up there" was looking after us. Those Japs could easily have shot us out of the air on any one of those first passes. But they didn't and we gave them no quarter. On the next pass I raked the boat with the grease-gun and hit a couple of them. On the next pass I killed the rest of the six on the boat. The other five were in the water and the boat was now floundering.

Off in the distance we could see an American Navy vessel headed north. We flew out with the intention of having them pick up the Japs in the water. As we approached we could see it was a Navy destroyer and as we swung by I could see a sailor with a twin 40mm antiaircraft gun tracking us! They weren't taking any chances. By hand signals, we indicated we wanted them to go over and pick up the five survivors. After several tries and a few minutes' delay (they were getting permission to leave the convoy on its way to Mindoro), the DD changed course and closed on the now half-sunk sailboat. When they saw the Japs in the water, they proceeded to pick them up. It took them some time as several of the Japs didn't want to be picked up. Finally when all five were on the fantail, we wagged our wings and flew back to Dipolog. It had been an interesting afternoon. Later back at Dipolog we had the picture of a sinking sailing banca painted on the side of the engine cowling to "record the kill" for the "Guerrilla Air Force." Kellet was really proud of that plane.

Back in Dipolog things were back to routine. The extra troops had been sent home, and there was no longer any threat to our treasury at Dapitan, and our airfield was secure. Bongalos was getting homesick and asked if he could go back to his family in Siokon. He had been a faithful companion for many months, and I hated to see him go, but I couldn't refuse. He caught a sailing banca going south in the next couple of days. I never saw Bongalos again.

On April 23 I received orders from Fertig to return to Dansalan and assume my duties as G-3 for the 10th Military District. I sent most of my baggage by truck to Misamis, then by launch and truck to Dansalan. Captain Killet and I flew back in the L-5. I never tired of looking down on the wooded hills and canyons as we skirted around north Zamboanga and Misamis with the 8,000 foot peaks of Mt. Dapiak and Mt. Malindang off to the west. Out across Iligan Bay I could see some of the reefs and shoals that used to give us so many rough crossings.

Back at Dansalan I found quarters in one of the buildings of old Camp Keithley. My G-3 office was already established and I had several Filipino officer assistants and a staff of eight. I saw Connie and she advised that she had been assigned to the medical unit at the 10th Military District headquarters. I was glad to see her again; I had last seen her just before I left for Dipolog back in early March.

Things were developing at a fast pace in Mindanao. As provinces were liberated from the Japanese, civil affairs military government units were moving in and the provinces were being turned over to representatives of the Philippine government. Guerrilla units in those areas were being integrated into the new Philippine Army. Misamis was being turned over, as was Zamboanga and Lanao.

On April 25 Colonel Fertig asked me if I would be interested in going to southern Cotabato to take command of a regiment being reactivated by the Philippine Army and help them flush the Japs out of the hills in the interior of Cotabato. After sleeping on the offer overnight, I concluded that my luck might be wearing thin. I decided to go back to the States. Colonel Fertig understood and issued orders for me to fly out to Leyte. I had been in the Philippines so long that it seemed strange that I would soon be leaving. After an emotional parting with Connie, I flew out by C-47 to Leyte on

April 30, 1945. I was closing a chapter of my life. It had been a long four years, and I felt like I was leaving home. At the time I had no idea that I would ever be back in the Philippines again. I had made a lot of friends in the Islands, but I had also lost a lot of friends and fellow officers. I did feel, however, that I had evened up the score somewhat with the Imperial Japanese Forces. Directly or indirectly I had eliminated 150 to 160 of their troops and in addition, accounted for 10 or 15 captured and sent to higher headquarters for interrogation. I felt I could now close the chapter with the satisfaction that I had fulfilled my promise to my fallen comrades.

16. Home—and Back to the Philippines

DURING the several weeks in Leyte, May, 1945, Major Thomas and I borrowed a B-25 and flew up to Manila to see the city. We contacted an old girlfriend of mine, Tropy O'Campo, who invited us to stay at her parents' home for a few days. Her father was with the police department of Manila at that time.

We visited the old walled city, Fort Santiago, the Escotta, and all the bombed-out parts of Manila, including the Army & Navy Club and the Manila Hotel. Very little had been cleaned up at that early date, and there were still munitions, smoldering ruins, and parts of bodies scattered around in the tunnels of the Walled City.

In June, I talked my way onto the troopship USS *President Grant* and took the long way home via Ulithi Atoll, Honolulu, and a train trip across the United States by way of New Orleans to end up at Fort Mead, Maryland. In spite of being a P.O.W. and having been overseas for four years, I was processed through without any physical exam or debriefing of any kind. I was offered a commission in the regular army with the rank of lieutenant colonel. I declined and went on six months' terminal leave with full pay and allowances.

On the train trip from Washington, D.C., to Lynchburg, Virginia, after a four-year absence, I fell asleep, missed my stop in Lynchburg, and had to catch a shift-train back from Danville, Virginia. I arrived home by taxi at 4:30 in the morning! After a couple of weeks at home I went to the Army rest camp at the Grove Park Inn in Asheville, N.C., where I was processed out into the Army Reserve. I began writing a book and, after a number of weeks in Lynchburg and at Sea Island, Georgia, as the guest of a friend, I went to New York City to see if I could sell my story. I visited Curtis Publishing Company and while they were not interested in my story they offered me a job in the advertising department of their new magazine, *Holiday*. I was in New York on V-J Day.

In training at the Curtis home office in Philadelphia I met my future bride, Mary Van Cott, who was at that time working in the copy service department. We were married about six months later in her hometown of Sea Cliff, Long Island. For the next six months I commuted about two hours into the city from Oyster Bay and later Freeport, Long Island. In the meantime, I was discovering that I was not suited to pounding the pavement of the canyons of New York City to sell advertising space in a magazine! Looking for a way out, I heard that Kenneth Day, president of the Philippine Refining Company was in town. I called on him and was hired to go back to the Philippines to buy copra in Mindanao for the new coconut oil mill they were building in Manila. Kenneth figured that, with my knowledge of Mindanao and my friends there, I could learn the copra business in a hurry and do a good job for the company. For me it was an opportunity to learn a new business, travel the world with my bride, and visit the old stamping grounds in Mindanao.

In 1946 we boarded the American President Lines' SS President Polk in New York for a fabulous trip. The other passengers thought we were on our honeymoon and called us "The Honeymooners." But we really were not, as we had been on our honeymoon in Bermuda. We sailed to Manila by way of Havana, the Panama Canal, Los Angeles, San Francisco (a ten-day stopover for Christmas), Shanghai, Hong Kong, and finally Manila. It was a most enjoyable trip of about 35 or 40 days and really qualified as a second honeymoon.

After a week or so in Manila, we took the Philippine Inter-Island steamer SS *Mayon* for a three-day trip to Cebu City, on the island of Cebu, where we would live for the next year. My job was to commute to Mindanao by light plane or on the company-owned 45-foot launch *TP-222* to buy copra from the Chinese or Filipino agents for shipment to our warehouse in Cebu, to the Manila mill, or for shipment to other mills in the Dutch East Indies or South Africa owned by our parent company Unilever Ltd. and Unilever, N.V.

On my trips, Mary went with me, making for a most enjoyable year. The trip to north Mindanao was about a two and half hour flight by light plane over water. We would take off from the Cebu airport, head south, and climb to 5,000 feet. By the time we had done this, we were halfway to Mindanao. If we had an engine failure, our glide patterns would put us in north Mindanao where we could land on almost any road in an emergency. The trip to north Mindanao by launch was a ten-hour affair, and we always left about midnight which put us in north Mindanao about mid-morning. The boat carried a captain, a crew of four or five, and we slept either in the cabin below decks or on the sofa in the wheelhouse saloon. In north Mindanao we either stayed on the launch or with Filipino friends ashore. Many times I stayed on board the Dutch, Norwegian, or British ships that I was loading with copra.

I was able to see many of my former comrades in the guerrillas and visited all the old battle grounds at Misamis, Malabang, Dipolog, and most of the other towns and cities in Mindanao. The Cota in Misamis had been rebuilt and was occupied by a unit of the Philippine Army. The airfields at

Labo and Dipolog were being used by the Philippine Air Lines. The roads we had rebuilt were still being used. Mr. Juridini, my Spanish friend from Misamis, was now living in Plaridel and I stopped for dinner with him many times. The Ozamis girls were still in the big hacienda at Jiminez, and we stayed there many times. Pedro Celdran was living in Mr. Barica's big house on Baliangao Bay and was our copra agent in that area. Jesus Montalvan was our agent in Oroquieta as was the Ozamis family in Jimenez. Colonel Hedges was gone from Iligan, but several of my former G-3 staff lived in the area and we talked over old times for many hours.

After our copra agents had been well established in Mindanao, Negros, Bohol, and Cebu, Mary and I moved up to Manila to be where I was to be assistant to the plant manager and to buy copra there. Our first son, Don, was born in Manila in June, 1948. We spent an enjoyable two years in Manila with several trips to the vacation city of Baguio. I traveled throughout Luzon to Bataan, to Fort Stotsenberg (now Clark Field), Cabanatuan, Lake Taal, and all the old places I had visited before the war as a lieutenant with the 26th Cavalry.

In 1950 we returned to the States on six months' leave. Kenneth Day was very generous, and I think the best boss I have ever had. Mary, Don and I sailed from Manila on the French liner *La Marseillaise* for France by way of Saigon, Singapore, Colombo, Djibouti, Suez, Port Said, Alexandria, and Marseilles. Again we had a fabulous 30-day cruise, then a stay on the French Riviera, in Paris, and home to New York on the *Queen Elizabeth*. We had circumnavigated the globe by boat, largely due to the generosity of Kenneth Day.

Conditions in the Philippines in 1950 were deteriorating and the "Huks" were very strong in Luzon. "Huk," short for "Hukbalahap," the acronym for the Hukbong Bayan Laban Sa Hapon or People's Anti-Japanese Resistance Army, in World War II killed an estimated 5,000 Japanese and liquidated some 20,000 of its Filipino rivals. The Huks are now the new People's Liberation Army. Therefore we decided not to renew our contract with Unilever Ltd. and I hired on at Procter and Gamble as a buyer of fats and oils. My second son, Charles, was born in Cincinnati on August 7, 1951. I spent the next 18 years with P & G, continued in the Army Reserve, and in 1969 resigned from P & G and went into the real estate business in Dallas. In 1972 we sold out and I retired at the age of 54. In 1978 I retired from the Army Reserve as a colonel.

While I was unwilling to take my family back to the Philippines in 1951 because of the political unrest, I have always had a soft place in my heart for the Philippines and the Filipino people. I continue to keep a close contact with events and developments in the Islands and my wife and I went back to the Islands in 1980 and 1981. Again we visited Manila, Baguio, Zamboanga, Bataan, Fort Stotsenberg, Lake Taal, and central Luzon. Those trips were enjoyable. Since about the time of the ouster of President Marcos, the Philippines have fallen on hard times. A considerable percentage of the population has taken a dislike to Americans and that has made the prospect of visiting the Islands unattractive. The United States military alliance with the Philippine government has ended and our bases at Subic Bay and Clark Field have been closed.

It is hoped that reason and intelligence will prevail and the Philippine government and the Filipino people will again restore the warm and friendly relations that have always existed between our countries since the Philippines became a commonwealth in the early 1900s and an independent country in 1946.

Index